Rev. D.M. Canright

Life of
Ellen White

By D.M. Canright

© 2005 by Gene Steffanson,
Revisions and additions.
All rights reserved.

The Great Controversy of 1858 Between God & Man, Christ &
Satan, H.L. Hastings & Ellen G. White
www.greatcontroversy.info

An Inquiry into the True Religion

Concise History of the Church

Stories of Children in the Bible

Bible Stories for Young People

WWW.LIFEOFELLENWHITE.COM

Imposture shrinks from light,
   And dreads the curious eye;
But sacred truths the test invite,
   They bid us search and try.
O may we still maintain
   A meek, inquiring mind,
Assured we shall not search in vain,
   But hidden treasures find.
With understanding blessed,
   Created to be free,
Our faith on man we dare not rest,
   We trust alone in Thee.
--Anonymous

Contents

Preface
    Why I Once Believed Mrs. White Inspired
    My Present Standing
Introduction   1
    Swedenborg
    Ann Lee and the Shakers
    Mrs. Joanna Southcott
    Joseph Smith and the Mormons
    Mrs. Eddy and Christian Science
    "Pastor" Russell
    Alexander Dowie
The Great Denominational Test   9
Claims Made For Her Writings   13
    As Inspired as the Bible
    Her Writings All Inspired by the Holy Ghost
    Mrs. White's Bible Seventeen Times as Large
        As God's Bible
Brief Sketch of Her Life   19
Where Now is Their "Spirit of Prophecy"?   48
Erroneous Views Concerning the Sanctuary   50
The Shut Door, or, Probation for Sinners Ended
    Oct. 22, 1844   53
    Elder Joseph Bates; His great Influence Upon
        Elder White and His Wife   56
    Early Adventists Teach the Shut Door
    Their Denial of These Plain Facts
    How the Shut Door was Opened
    Seventh-day Adventists Hold Key to Door of Mercy
    Signed Testimony
    The Results of Fanaticism

Damaging Writings Suppressed	77
A Deliberate Deception	
Still At It	
Philosophy of Her Visions	92
A Great Plagiarist	104
The Charge of Plagiarism	
Dr. Stewart's Comparison	
Used Her Gift to Get Money	115
Her High Claims Disproved	118
First Visions Childish	123
A Historical Blunder About the Two Herods	
Editor Smith Rejected Her Testimonies	126
Her Prophecies Fail	131
Predicitons About the Civil War	
Claimed to Reveal Secret Sins	138
Influenced to Write Testimonies	143
Rebuked the Wrong Man	
What Called It Out	
Led by Dr. Kellogg to Deny the	
Resurrection of the Body	
Broke the Sabbath Nine Years	150
The Reform Dress	153
A Short Dress with Pants	
Her False Vision About the Planets	157
"Give Sunday to the Lord"	161
Conclusion	165

Preface

Mrs. E.G. White, the prophetess, leader, and chief founder of the Seventh-day Adventist Church, claimed to be divinely inspired by God the same as were the prophets of the Bible. Defining her position, she says: "In ancient times God spoke to men by the mouth of prophets and apostles. In these days he speaks to them by the testimonies of his Spirit." (*Testimonies for the Church*, Vol. IV., p. 148; Vol. V., p. 661; No. 88, p. 189) that is, by her through her writings.

Every line she wrote, whether in articles, letters, testimonies, or books, she claimed was dictated to her by the Holy Ghost, and hence must be infallible.

Her people accept and defend these claims strongly. Her writings are read in their churches, taught in their schools, and preached by their ministers the same as the Holy Scriptures. Their church stands or falls with her claims. This they freely admit. She stands related to her people the same as Mohammed to the Mohammedans, Joseph Smith to the Mormons, Ann Lee to the Shakers, and Mrs. Eddy to the Christian Scientists.

Hence these high claims are a subject for fair investigation, to which her followers, who have freely criticized other claimants to divine inspiration, can not reasonably object. They have published several books bearing on her life and work, in which they have gathered together and construed everything possible in her favor. From reading these books one would never know that she ever made a mistake, plagiarized, practiced deception, or wrote alleged inspired writings which had to be suppressed. In narrating the lives of inspired men God does not thus cover up their failures and pass by their mistakes and shortcomings.

The public, therefore, has a right to know the other side of the life of Mrs. White.

The writer is perhaps better qualified to give the facts regarding that phase of her life than any other person living, as he united with her people almost at their beginning, now nearly sixty years ago, when they numbered only about five thousand. He has all the writings of Mrs. White in those early days. Some of the most damaging of these have been suppressed. Neither the public nor their own people, except a few officials, know of these old "revelations." His intimate association with Mrs. White gave him an opportunity to know and observe her as no one without such association could possibly have.

WHY I ONCE BELIEVED MRS. WHITE INSPIRED

I once accepted Mrs. White's claim to inspiration for the same reason that most of her followers do. I first accepted the Sabbath, and then other points of the faith, until I came to believe it all.

Once among and of them, I found all stating in strong terms that Mrs. White was inspired of God. I supposed they knew, and so took their word for it; and that is what all the others do as they come in, deny it as they may.

I soon found that her revelations were so connected with the whole history and belief of her church that I could not consistently separate them any more than a person could be a Mormon and not believe in Joseph Smith, or a Christian Scientist and not believe in Mrs. Eddy.

I believed the other doctrines so firmly that I swallowed the visions with the rest, and that is what all do.

When I began to have suspicions about the visions I found the pressure so strong that I feared to express them, or even to admit them to myself. All said such doubts were of the devil and would lead to a rejection of the truth and then to ruin. So I dared not entertain them nor investigate the matter; and this is the way it is with others.

I saw that all who expressed any doubts about the visions were immediately branded as "rebels," as "in the dark," "led by Satan," "infidels," etc.

Having no faith in any other doctrine or people, I did not know what to do nor where to go. So I tried to believe the visions and go along just as thousands of them do when really they are in doubt about them all the time. This leads them to practice deception, and pretend publicly to believe what inwardly they do not believe, or at best what they doubt. See Uriah Smith's case in the chapter dealing with his view.

Over forty years ago, in my early ministry and while yet a firm believer in all the Seventh-day Adventist doctrines, I wrote a strong defense of Mrs. White. During all the years since, nothing so forcible has been produced by any of her defenders. This is proved by the fact that it has been copied by them in her defense, but omitting my name. Also in their writings against me they quote this as contradicting what I now say. I do not blame them; but my answer is this: "A wise man changes his mind seldom, a fool never."

At the time I wrote that defense of Mrs. White, forty years ago, I had never seen a copy of her early visions contained in *A Word to the Little Flock*, 1847, and in *Present Truth*, 1849 and 1850; nor Elder Bates' pamphlets at the same date. They had been so effectively suppressed that I did not know they ever existed. These contain the most damaging evidence against her inspiration. All these came into my hands later. As the years went by, other evidences kept gradually accumulating, until I was compelled to change my mind.

During his early years in Parliament, Mr. Gladstone, the great statesman of England, made speeches strongly defending the side to which he belonged. Later he changed his views and joined the opposing side. Then a member of his old party arose and read one of Mr. Gladstone's speeches strongly condemning the views he now advocated. At the close all eyes were on Mr. Gladstone. What could he say? He arose slowly and said: "That was a long while ago, and many things have happened since." That was all. The House cheered him lustily. He had effectually answered his opponent. My answer to the Adventists is the same: "That was a long while ago, and many things have happened since."

The facts presented in this book give some of the reasons why I gave up faith in Mrs. White's claim to inspiration. The facts are indisputable; the conclusions based on them must, therefore, in the very nature of the case, be inevitable.

In performing this task, the writer, knowing the frailties of human nature, has used as mild language and shown as much charity as the facts in the case would permit. But, knowing the errors and deceptions which have been connected with Mrs. White and her work, he has felt it a duty which he owed to the Christian world to state the facts.

—The Author.

My Present Standing

Since I withdrew from the Adventists, over thirty years ago, they have continued to report that I have regretted leaving them, have tried to get back again, have repudiated my book which I wrote, and have confessed that I am now a lost man. There has never been a word of truth in any of these reports. **I expect them to report that I recanted on my deathbed.** All this is done to hinder the influence of my books. I now reaffirm all that I have written in my books and tracts against that doctrine.

Several Adventist ministers have rendered valuable aid in preparing these pages. Once they were believers in Mrs. White's divine inspiration, but plain facts finally compelled them to renounce faith in her dreams.

—D.M. Canright,
Pastor Emeritus,
Berean Baptist Church,
Grand Rapids, Mich.

Introduction

Seventh-day Adventists regard Mrs. White as a prophet, and her writings as inspired. They make long arguments from the Bible to prove that there should be "gifts" in the church, the same as do Mormons, Shakers, and others for their churches. They do this to substantiate their claim for the one "gift of prophecy," which they say was possessed by Mrs. White.

The Bible says: "Beware of false prophets." (Matt. 7:15.) "There shall arise false Christs and false prophets." (Matt. 24:24.) "Believe not every spirit, but try the spirits: . . .because many false prophets are gone out into the world." (1 John 4:1.)

In every generation many have arisen claiming to be prophets. All have found followers, more or less. All they had to do was to firmly believe in themselves, and make extravagant claims, and they soon had followers. Mohammed, who arose in the sixth century A.D., with his two hundred millions of followers today, is a notable example. Let us notice a few prominent ones near our own times.

SWEDENBORG

Emanuel Swedenborg was born in Stockholm, Sweden, 1688, and died in 1772. He was a favorite with the king and royal family. He was of the purest character, and devoutly religious. Not a stain rests on his moral character.

At the age of fifty-five, according to *Schaff-Herzog's Encyclopedia*, from which we condense this sketch, he began to have visions of heaven, hell, angels, and the spiritual world. He says:

"I have been called to a holy office by the Lord himself, who most mercifully appeared to me, his servant, in the year 1743, when he opened my sight into the spiritual world and enabled me to converse with spirits and angels." Exactly like what Mrs. White claimed. This work he continued for thirty years, during which time he wrote about thirty inspired volumes. He made some remarkable predictions, which his followers claim were exactly fulfilled.

He founded a new church based upon his revelations. The Bible is sacredly taught, and holy living enjoined. The church has steadily increased till it has societies in all parts of the world. They publish several periodicals, besides many books. His followers believe in him just as implicitly as do Mrs. White's followers in her, and are very zealous in propagating their faith.

ANN LEE AND THE SHAKERS

The Shakers are so well known in America that little need be said about them. Ann Lee, their leader, was born in England in 1736; died, 1784. Like Mrs. White, "She received no education." She joined a society the members of which were having remarkable religious exercises, and soon began "to have visions and make revelations," which, like Mrs. White, she called "testimonies."

"Henceforth she claimed to be directed by revelations and visions." (*Schaff-Herzog Encyclopedia,* article "Ann Lee".) She was accepted as leader and as "the second appearing of Christ."

Like Mrs. White, she required "a peculiar kind of dress," and "opposed war and the use of pork." (*Johnson's Cyclopedia,* article "Shakers".) Her followers have no intercourse with other churches, and are renowned for their purity and devotion.

In proof of Mrs. White's inspiration, Adventists cite the high moral and religious tone of her writings. They say her revelations must either be of God or Satan. If of Satan, they would not teach such purity or holiness. The same reasoning will prove Mrs. Lee also a true prophetess, for she exceeds Mrs. White in this line, so that "Shaker" has become a synonym for honesty.

Introduction

Mrs. Joanna Southcott

This noted woman was born in England in 1750, of poor parents, and was wholly uneducated. She worked as a domestic servant till over forty years of age. She joined the Methodists in 1790. In 1792 she announced herself as a prophetess, and "published numerous pamphlets setting forth her revelations." (*Johnson's Cyclopedia,* article "Southcott".)

She had trances the same as Mrs. White, and announced the speedy advent of Christ. (See *Encyclopedia Americana,* article "Southcott.") She carried on a lucrative trade in the sale of her books, as did Mrs. White. Strange as it may appear, many leading ministers in England believed in her, and thousands became her followers, until in a few years they numbered over one hundred thousand. "The faith of her followers," says the *Encyclopedia Americana,* "rose to enthusiasm."

She "regarded herself as the bride of the Lamb, and declared herself, when sixty-four years of age, pregnant with the true Messiah, the 'second Shiloh,' whom she would bear Oct. 19, 1814...Joanna died in her self-delusion Dec. 27, 1814; but her followers, who at one time numbered a hundred thousand, continued till 1831 to observe the Jewish Sabbath." (*Schaff-Herzog Encyclopedia.*) "A post-mortem examination showed that she had been suffering from dropsy." (*Johnson's Cyclopedia.*) "Death put an end to both her hopes and fears. With her followers, however, it was otherwise; and, although for a time confounded by her decease, which they could scarcely believe to be real, her speedy resurrection was confidently anticipated. In this persuasion they lived and died, nor is her sect yet extinct." (*Encyclopedia Americana,* article "Southcott".)

Mrs. White claimed her gift to be the "testimony of Jesus" spoken of in Rev. 12:17, while Mrs. Southcott claimed to be the "woman" spoken of in verses 1 and 2 of the same chapter. Mrs. Southcott wrote *A Book of Wonders,* while Mrs. White wrote a book called *The Great Controversy.** Mrs. White's followers claim

---

* See *The Great Controversy of 1858 Between God & Man, Christ & Satan,* H.L. Hastings & Ellen G. White, Dixie Press, www.greatcontroversy.info

the latter to be the most wonderful book of the age. They have sold it by the carload, Mrs. White receiving a large royalty. A recent biographer of Mrs. Southcott says of her books: "She found the business very profitable,...and proceeded to rake in the money by selling her prophecies." This is exactly what Mrs. White did.

Mrs. Southcott claimed to be called to "seal" the hundred and forty and four thousand of Rev. 7:1-4. Mrs. White claimed to have a message to seal the same hundred and forty and four thousand with the Sabbath.

She seems to have patterned very much after Mrs. Southcott in various ways. The following from *Chambers' Encyclopedia* (article "Southcott") is also applicable to Mrs. White and her followers: "The history of Joanna Southcott herself has not much in it that is marvelous; but the influence which she exercised over others may well be deemed so, and the infatuation of her followers is hard to be understood, particularly when it is considered that some of them were men of some intelligence and of cultivated mind. Probably the secret of her influence lay in the fact that the poor creature was in earnest about her own delusions. So few people in the world are really so, that they are always liable to be enslaved by others who have convictions of any kind, however grotesque. On her death-bed Joanna said: 'If I have been misled, it has been by some spirit, good or evil.' Poor Joanna never suspected that the spirit which played such vagaries was her own."

Just so of Mrs. White. It is marvelous that, with all the proof of her failures, intelligent men are still led by her. But the cases of Joanna, of Ann Lee and others, help us to solve this one. All have earnestly believed in their own inspiration, and this fact has convinced others. Here notice the terrible tenacity of fanaticism when once started. When Joanna died we would have supposed that all sane persons would have given it up, but they adjusted it in some way, and went right on.

So with the followers of Mrs. White. No matter what blunders and failures she made, they fix them up and go right on.

Introduction

Joseph Smith and the Mormons

This prophet and his visions and revelations are so well known that we mention them but briefly. Smith was born in 1805, and died in 1844, the year Mrs. White began to have her revelations. He came out in a great religious awakening, as did Mrs. White in the Advent movement of 1843-4. Like Mrs. White, he was uneducated, poverty poor, and unknown. In 1823 he began to have "visions" and "revelations," and to see and talk with angels. The second advent of Christ was at hand, he said, hence the name, "Latter-day Saints." His mission was to introduce "the new dispensation." His followers are the "saints," and all other churches are "heathen," or Gentiles. Mrs. White's followers, likewise, are the saints; all other churches are "Babylon" and apostate.

As for having the "gifts" in the church, the Mormons far excel the Adventists. Besides having a prophet, they have apostles work many miracles, as they strongly assert; have the gift of tongues, and can show, they claim, many predictions strikingly fulfilled. They also have a new Bible, a new revelation, have started a new sect, and will have nothing to do with others, but proselyte from all.

The Mormons began in 1831, only about fifteen years before Seventh-day Adventists did; but they now number over five hundred thousand, four times what Adventists do. They are increasing more rapidly than Adventists, who "point with pride" to their growth as proof that God is with them.

Seventh-day Adventists claim that they must be the true church because they have a prophet and are persecuted; but Mormons have a prophet and have been persecuted a thousand-fold more. Smith and others were killed; many have been whipped, tarred and feathered, rotten-egged, stoned, mobbed, run out of town and outlawed. So they must be the true church! In comparison, Seventh-day Adventists have suffered little. They have little idea what persecution is, though all along they have seemed anxious to pose as martyrs.

Mrs. Eddy and Christian Science

It is not our purpose in these few lines to discuss the character of either Mrs. Eddy or Christian Science, but simply to show how easily people are led and ruled by professed inspired prophets of God, no matter what they teach.

Mrs. Eddy was born July 16, 1821, in New Hampshire, and died Dec. 3, 1910, near Boston, being nearly ninety years old. Mrs. White was born in 1827, and died in 1915, at the age of nearly eighty-eight. Both lived during practically the same period of time. The religious systems of the two, however, are exactly the opposite. In Mrs. White's revelations the devil is a large, portly man with flesh and bones; the redeemed saints have wings, and fly like birds, live in silver houses, and in a world where gold trees with silver branches bear fruit. Everything is very literal and very material. In the final destruction God tortures the wicked to the limit. Speaking of the destruction of the wicked, she says: "I saw that...some were many days consuming, and just as long as there was a portion of them unconsumed, all the sense of suffering remained." (*Early Writings*, p. 154, ed. 1882.)

With Mrs. Eddy there is no such thing as matter; all is only mind, spirit, principle. There is no personal God, no devil, no angels, no sin, no evil, no disease, no hell, no eternal punishment, no lost souls, Jesus only human, no resurrection, no second advent, no day of judgment, parts of the Bible only myths and misleading, God never answers prayer. Yet these two prophets; with such opposite theories, find ready followers. The disciples of each believe their own prophet with equal devotion, and the writings of each as inspired and infallible. These writings are their Bibles, telling what God's Bible means. Christian Scientists, as a class, stand high morally and socially. In these respects they excel Adventists. If teaching purity of life proved Mrs. White to be an inspired prophet of God, it proves the same thing for Mrs. Eddy.

The fact is that neither of these women leaders was inspired either by God or by Satan, but by their own inherited highly wrought religious reveries molded by the dominant influences

INTRODUCTION

which came into their lives. It is not necessary to believe that Mrs. Eddy was dishonest. She was simply a religious enthusiast, carried away with her own mental delusions, the same as Mrs. White. Adventists point to their success as proof that Mrs. White was a true prophet. But the believers in Mrs. Eddy outnumber them ten to one, though beginning their work over twenty years later.

"PASTOR" RUSSELL

Speaking of Mr. Russell shortly after his death, the *New York Watchman-Examiner* of Nov. 9, 1916, says: "When Charles T. Russell, who styled himself 'Pastor' Russell, died, a remarkable man passed out of the world. We should unhesitatingly place him in a class with Alexander Dowie, and Joseph Smith, the founder of Mormonism.

"Keen-witted, eloquent and a master dialectician, he played the mountebank so successfully that he gathered multitudes of followers, in many instances deceiving even God's elect. He built around him a great organization of men and women, who responded to his leadership as the Mormons obey the commands of their prophet. A stream of gold poured into his coffers, and was used in a world-wide advertising propaganda.

"He was without training, and was never ordained to the ministry, and yet he spoke to unnumbered multitudes by voice and pen, and won to his erratic views many from all denominations. This success came despite the fact that his own life was a reproach to Christianity. It still seems to be true that men like to be fooled, and 'Pastor' Russell fooled multitudes.

"It is announced that his death will in nowise interfere with the propagation of his views, and the promotion of 'Millennial Dawnism.' Indeed, it is highly probable that the fanaticism that possessed many of his followers will manifest itself in a new propaganda. Already thousands of women tread the streets of our great cities distributing the literature of Russellism. People are hungry for the knowledge of the unknown and mysterious future. Mr. Russell capitalized this deep longing of the human heart, and with unparalleled dogmatism gave the most minute and exact information concerning the unborn future."

Mr. Russell set various times for the world to come to an end, the latest being in 1914. In October of that year he said the "times of the Gentiles" would be fulfilled. His followers claim that he was the greatest man that has lived since the apostles, and that his sect is the only true church. All others are Babylon.

Mr. Russell lived right along at the same time with Mrs. White and Mrs. Eddy. The followers of each one accept their leader as the only infallible oracle of God. Can they all be right?

ALEXANDER DOWIE

Here in our day was another claimant to divine inspiration - the second Elijah. For years he attracted wide notoriety. It was claimed that he performed hundreds of miraculous cures. The devotion and enthusiasm of his followers were unbounded. Money flowed in freely. Like Mrs. White and Mrs. Eddy, he was dogmatic and arbitrary. His word was law. He required an austere religious life, exceeding even Mrs. White. The sect still lives on at Zion City, Chicago.

Notice what a crop of false prophets the last century has produced. It seems to be in the air of the age. Not one of those here mentioned, except Mrs. White, is regarded by Seventh-day Adventists as a true prophet. They call Swedenborg a Spiritualist. Joseph Smith they regard as an impostor, and his writings as a fabrication. Against Mrs. Eddy and Christian Science they have written extensively. Against "Pastor" Russell and his teachings they publish a work entitled *The Darkness of Millennial Dawn*. None passes muster with them. All are false. The only true prophet of modern times is their own.

The object of this book is to investigate the claims of Mrs. White, the prophetess of Seventh-day Adventists, and, from documentary evidence, plain facts and incontrovertible proofs, allow the reader to judge for himself whether or not she should be classed with the other false prophets of the age here noted.

The Great Denominational Test

"Seventh-day Adventists have no creed but the Bible." This statement is made over and over again in their publications intended for public distribution.

Likewise they say: "The Bible is its own expositor." "One text explains another."

This all sounds well, but upon examination both statements are shown to be false.

In the first place, Seventh-day Adventists have a creed, the same as do other denominations, and have published this ever since 1872. They call it the "Fundamental Principles of Seventh-day Adventists." Its opening words are: "Seventh-day Adventists have no creed but the Bible; but they hold to certain well-defined points of faith." And then they at once proceed to define these "points of faith." What is this but a creed?

Webster defines creed as *"an authoritative summary or formula of those articles of Christian faith which are considered essential."* Opening the disciplines of the various orthodox churches, such as Methodists, Baptists and Presbyterians, we find each beginning its articles of faith thus: "We believe." Then follows what they believe. Adventists say that all these churches have a creed, but they themselves have no creed. But their "Fundamental Principles" begin in the same way, thus: "We believe;" and then follow their twenty-nine articles of faith, telling what they believe. Hence, for them to say they have no creed, but other churches have, is a deception.

But the worst feature about this creed is that it does not contain their chief article of faith - that which they regard as the greatest essential of all. Strange as it may seem, this is omitted. Their greatest deception in this matter is not in having a formulated creed when they say they have no creed, but in failing to insert in their formulated creed the one paramount article of their faith.

The third article of their published creed says they hold: "That the Holy Scriptures of the Old and New Testament were given by inspiration of God, contain a full revelation of His will to man, and are the only infallible rule of faith and practice."

This again sounds well; but it is false, absolutely false. Seventh-day Adventists do not believe that the Scriptures of the Old and New Testaments contain the full revelation of God's will to man, neither do they take these Scriptures as their "only infallible rule of faith and practice," for they hold that the writings of their prophetess, Mrs. E.G. White, are also given by inspiration of God; that these writings contain a fuller revelation of God's will to man, and that they are infallible. And, what is more, they make faith in these writings a test of faith and fellowship in their church. All this is susceptible of the clearest proof.

Over and over Mrs. White claimed her writings to be inspired of God, and placed them on a level with the Bible. She says: "I took the precious Bible, and surrounded it with the several Testimonies for the Church, given for the people of God. 'Here,' said I, 'the cases of nearly all are met.'" (*Testimonies*, Vol. 2, p. 605; Vol. 5, p. 664.)

According to 2 Tim. 3:16,17, the Bible alone is a sufficient guide to heaven, thoroughly furnishing the man of God unto all good works. But Mrs. White adds her writings to the Bible; surrounds it with them, in fact. With the two thus placed together, she says "the cases of *nearly all* are met." The Bible alone, therefore, must be better; for that meets the cases of all.

The claim of infallibility was set up for Mrs. White's writings in 1911. In that year they declared her writings to be "the only infallible interpreter of Bible principles" (*The Mark of the Beast*, by G.A. Irwin, p. 1.)

With them, therefore, the Bible is not their only creed, it is not its own expositor, neither is it their only infallible rule of faith and practice. On the contrary, faith in Mrs. White and her writings is the great thing - the chief, but unpublished, article of faith. It is not an uncommon thing to hear their older members say, "If I gave up faith in Mrs. White, I would give up everything." This shows that everything in this church is built on her. To disbelieve in her is the greatest of heresies, and at once brands one as an apostate.

Before uniting with the church one hears little or nothing about Mrs. White; but, after uniting, one hears her quoted constantly as authority upon everything - doctrine, diet, dress, and discipline. Those who at first do not accept her visions, Mrs. White says, "must not be set aside, but long patience and brotherly love should be exercised toward then until they find their position and become established for or against." But, "if they fight against the visions," then, she says, "the church may know that they are not right." (*Testimonies*, Vol. I., p. 328) This shows that in the end, according to Mrs. White's own writings, faith in her writings is made a test of faith and fellowship in this church.

Consequently, all along, not only church members, but whole churches, have been disfellowshipped for disbelief in Mrs. White's visions. To get rid of members who did not believe in her inspiration, whole churches have been summarily disbanded by church officials without their consent, and reorganized, faith in Mrs. White and her writings being made a test for entering the new organization. In October, 1913, their church in St. Louis, Mo., was disbanded in this way.

The last three questions asked those who desired to unite with the reorganized church were these:

"11. Do you believe that the remnant church must have the spirit of prophecy?

"12. Do you believe in the spirit of prophecy as vested in Mrs. E.G. White?

"13. Do you believe in health reform as taught in the Bible, and the spirit of prophecy?"

This is sufficient to show that "the Bible, and the Bible *only*," is not the creed of Seventh-day Adventists. It is the Bible and something else; it is the Bible and the writings of Mrs. White. It is not honest, therefore, for them to publish to the world that they have "no creed but the Bible." Neither is it honest, in publishing their creed, to omit that which is their chief article of faith and great denominational test. It is only fair that the public should know of their deception in this matter.

They are not as frank and honest in this respect as are the Mormons. The Mormons have a creed, formulated by Joseph Smith in 1841, and adopted later by their general conference, which they publish as their *Articles of Faith*. They do not hesitate to call this their creed. Neither do they in this creed suppress the fact that they believe in the *Book of Mormon*. Article VIII. Of this creed says: "We believe the Bible to be the word of God, as far as it is translated correctly, we also believe the Book of Mormon to be the word of God."

Why should not Seventh-day Adventists be as honest, and state in their creed that they believe the writings of Mrs. White to be the word of God? There must be something radically wrong with a denomination that will thus, with fair but false words and suppressed facts, attempt to deceive the innocent and unsuspecting public, and with a spiritual "gift" which requires so much deception to protect it.

Claims Made for Her Writings

AS INSPIRED AS THE BIBLE

Over and over, Seventh-day Adventists have given Mrs. White the highest possible endorsement. On Feb. 7, 1871, their General Conference passed the following resolution: "That we reaffirm our abiding confidence in the Testimonies of Sister White to the church, as the teaching of the Spirit of God." (*SDA Year Book for 1914*, p. 253.)

Again they say: "Our position on the Testimonies is like the keystone to the arch. Take that out, and there is no logical stopping place till all the special truths of the message are gone...Nothing is surer than this, that the message and the visions [of Mrs. White] belong together, and stand or fall together."(*Review and Herald Supplement*, Aug. 14, 1883.)

"The Spirit of Prophecy [Mrs. White's writings] is a fundamental part of this message...Since the rise of this message, this denomination has believed in the Spirit of Prophecy. We have preached it as widely as we have the Sabbath and other kindred truths, and believe it as thoroughly...To us it makes a vast difference whether one whom we have regarded from the rise of this message as being endowed with the prophetic gift is a prophet of God, or whether she is not." ("Statement by the General Conference Committee," May, 1906, pp. 10, 86.)

Notice that this church is built upon Mrs. White and her writings. They liken these writings to the keystone in the arch. The whole structure tumbles if that keystone is left out. Just so, the Seventh-day Adventist Church would fall if Mrs. White's writings were left out, they say, and truly, too. By their own confession, that church is not built upon Jesus Christ and the Bible, but upon Mrs. White and her writings.

The Protestant rule is, "*The Bible, and the Bible only, as the rule of faith and practice.*" Seventh-day Adventists do not abide by this rule, but add to the Bible the writings of Mrs. White, and make them superior to the Bible; the keystone to their whole system, without which it would fall. Hence, according to their own statement, if left with the Bible only, without her writings, their church would fall. On what, then, is their church founded? On Mrs. White's writings, visions and dreams.

Now read this from G.A. Irwin, many years president of their General Conference. On page 1 of a tract entitled *The Mark of the Beast* he says: "It is from the standpoint of the light that has come through the Spirit of Prophecy [Mrs. White's writings] that the question will be considered, believing as we do that the Spirit of Prophecy is the only infallible interpreter of Bible principles, since it is Christ through this agency giving the real meaning of his words."

Here we have an infallible female pope endorsed as such by that church. They claim for her exactly the same prerogative which the Catholic Church claims for the Pope; namely, that she is the only infallible interpreter of the Bible. No pope of Rome ever claimed more. The Mormons claim no more for Joseph Smith, nor Christian Scientists for Mrs. Eddy.

Now listen to the claim of inspiration and infallibility for Mrs. Eddy, as voiced in the *Christian Science Sentinel*, Nov. 4, 1916: "To grasp the real import of Christian Science, to gain some sense of its infinite scope, to realize its infallibility and render unquestioning obedience thereto, one must perceive it to be a revelation from God, hence unalterable truth. To believe in the inspiration of the Bible, and of *Science and Health with Key to the Scriptures* by Mrs. Eddy, is a step in the right direction...Furthermore, he recognizes the Discoverer and Founder of Christian Science as the true and only possible Leader of Christian Scientists."

Here are two women, both living at the same time, teaching exactly opposite religious theories, both claiming to be divinely inspired, and both declared infallible and the only true guide.

CLAIMS MADE FOR HER WRITINGS

Which shall we believe?

Editors and ministers of the Adventist Church urge the "testimonies" of Mrs. White upon their people constantly, in their sermons and church papers. They quote her more than they do the Bible, and with the same authority. Their ministers are required to study her writings with the Bible. Any interpretation she puts on a text, or any statement she makes on a subject, settles it beyond dispute. It is what God says, and that ends it.

Thus Uriah Smith, writing in 1868, before he got his eyes open to the facts, defending her visions, says: "We discard nothing that the visions have ever taught from beginning to end, from first to last." (*The Visions of Mrs. E.G. White*, p. 40.)

Here is another in the *Review and Herald*, Oct. 5, 1914: "As with the ancient prophets, the talking is done by the Holy Spirit through her vocal organs. The prophets spake as they were moved by the Holy Ghost."

Then again in the same paper, Aug. 26, 1915, is this: "Think you that he would choose an inferior mouthpiece through whom to instruct the remnant church? On the other hand, as it is the greatest crisis of all ages, we should naturally expect that the mouthpiece God would use for this period would be inferior to none in the past ages."

Language could not be stronger. Mrs. White was not inferior to any of the prophets of past ages. Hence she is equal to Moses, Isaiah, Daniel, Paul, and John the Revelator. This they teach constantly.

HER WRITINGS ALL INSPIRED BY THE HOLY GHOST

Now read what Mrs. White claims for her writings. Defining her position, she says: "In ancient times God spoke through the mouths of prophets and apostles. In these days he speaks to them by the Testimonies of his Spirit." (*Testimonies*, Vol. IV., p. 148; Vol. V., p. 661.)

Here she places herself on a level with all the Bible writers, both prophets and apostles. (See Heb. 1:1,2.) Anyone who rejects or opposes her writings is branded as a rebel fighting against God. Thus she says: "If you lessen the confidence of

God's people in the testimonies he has sent them, you are rebelling against God as certainly as were Korah, Dathan and Abirum." (*Testimonies,* Vol. V., p. 66.)

Here she classes herself in authority with Moses. From this it will be seen that her followers have made no greater claims for her than she made for herself. She claims that every line she writes, even in a private letter, is directly inspired by God - "the precious rays of light shining from the throne" (same book, p. 67.)

Of her own words she says: "It is God, and not an erring mortal, that has spoken." (*Testimonies,* Vol. III., p. 257.)

She states over and over that those who doubt or oppose her are fighting against God, sinning against the Holy Ghost. Thus: "fighting the Spirit of God. Those...who would break down our testimony, I saw, are not fighting against us, but against God." (p. 260.)

Again she says: "When I went to Colorado, I wrote many pages to be read at your camp meeting...God was speaking through clay. You might say this communication was only a letter. Yes, it was a letter, but prompted by the Spirit of God, to bring before your minds things that had been shown me.

"In these letters which I write,...I am presenting to you that which the Lord has presented to me. I do not write one article in the paper expressing merely my own ideas. They are what God has opened before me in vision - the precious rays of light shining from the throne." (*Testimonies*, Vol. V., pp. 63-67.)

Notice that she claims to be simply the mouthpiece for God. They are not her words, but God's words, the same as the Bible - God speaking through clay. All through her writings, designed especially for her own people, may be found expressions of this kind. In her books prepared for the public, however, all these expressions are carefully omitted.

Mrs. White's Bible Seventeen Times as Large as God's Bible

As given in the back part of *Life Sketches of Mrs. White*, her books comprise a total of 13,351 pages. A regular Teacher's Bible, good-sized print, contains 771 pages. It will be seen, therefore, that Mrs. White's inspired books are seventeen times as large as our Bible.

Their ministers study all these books the same as God's Bible. An editorial in the *Lake Union Herald*, Dec. 22, 1915, says: "We would urge all our people to study the *Testimonies* daily. Our workers, especially, should read them over and over again."

Here are alleged inspired writings, seventeen times as large as the Bible, to be read over and over again! To do this the ordinary person could read little else. Few Bible students read the Bible through in less than a year.

𝔅rief 𝔖ketch of 𝔥er 𝔏ife

Ellen G. White was born at Gorham, Maine, Nov. 26, 1827. Her maiden name was Harmon. When a child, her parents moved to Portland, Maine.

In her *Testimonies for the Church* (Vol. I., pp. 9-58), Mrs. White gives a lengthy account of her childhood, youth, conversion, and acceptance of Adventism under the preaching of William Miller.

Her parents and all the family were Methodists of the most zealous kind until disfellowshipped for their strong adherence to the time-setting doctrines of Mr. Miller.

When only nine years of age, becoming angry "at some trifle," as Mrs. White expresses it, a schoolgirl, running after her, threw a stone at her and broke her nose. The blow was so severe that it nearly killed her. She was disfigured for life. She lay unconscious for three weeks, and was not expected to live. (p. 10.)

When she began to recover and saw how disfigured she was, she wanted to die. She became melancholy, and avoided all company. She says: "My nervous system was prostrated." (p. 13.) After a time she tried to attend school again, but had to discontinue, as she could not study. So her school education never went beyond learning to read and write a little. (p. 13.)

In 1840, at the age of thirteen, she heard William Miller preach that the end of the world would come in 1843. She was terribly frightened, and thought she would be lost. (p. 15.) Returning home, she spent nearly all night in prayer and tears. (p. 16.) She continued in this hopeless condition for months. (p. 16.)

Then, at a Methodist camp meeting, she had a wonderful

conversion. (p. 18.) Here she saw many fall unconscious with the "power," as was common then. Here parents were with her there, and in full sympathy with these exercises.

Again, in 1842, she heard Miller prove that Christ would come in one short year. She was terribly frightened again. She says: "Condemnation rang in my ears day and night." (p. 23.) "I feared that I would lose my reason." (p. 25.) "Despair overwhelmed me. I frequently remained in prayer all night, groaning and trembling with inexpressible anguish." (p. 26.) This indicates her mental condition.

In dreams she went to heaven and met Jesus, and was relieved. (p. 28.) Then she attended prayer meeting and fell unconscious, and remained in this state all night. (p. 31.) This was often repeated. She seeks to give the impression that her exercises were all the work of the Spirit of God.

But were they? No; they were simply the result of her physical and mental condition, wrought upon by the religious excitements with which she was unfortunately surrounded. Miller's alarming predictions nearly unbalanced her hysterical mind in her feeble body. Later she herself confesses this. She says: "Could the truth have been presented to me as I now understand it, much perplexity and sorrow would have been spared me." (p. 25.)

She simply had a wrong conception of God and the simplicity of the gospel. That misconception never wholly left her. The idea of a severe God and his service runs all through her writings. It shows how completely she was influenced by her associates and the spiritual atmosphere surrounding her. Instead of the Spirit of God controlling her mind all her life as she supposed, it was her own spirit influenced by leading minds around her. The following pages will demonstrate this.

Now notice the difference in the conversion of her husband, Elder James White. The entire account of this is given by himself in just fourteen words. In *Life Sketches* (p. 15) he says: "At the age of fifteen I was baptized and united with the Christian church." That is all he says about it.

His father had been a Baptist deacon, then a member of the Christian church. Neither his parents, his church, nor his associ-

Brief Sketch of Her Life

ates were accustomed to such extreme religious exercises as Ellen Harmon's had been. But was not his conversion as genuine as hers? She never questioned it.

From 1840 to 1844, from the age of thirteen to seventeen, this little girl, feeble, sickly, uneducated, impressible, and abnormally religious and excitable, fell under the influence of Mr. Miller's lectures predicting the end of the world in 1843, then in 1844. Toward the last she attended these exciting meetings constantly, and believed without a question all he predicted. She says: "I believed the solemn words spoken by the servant of God." (p. 22.)

The effect on her weak, imaginative and unbalanced young mind was terrible. She said: "It seemed to me that my doom was fixed." (p. 28.)

Her parents and all the family accepted Miller's theories, which caused their separation from the Methodist Church.

Miller's prediction that the end would come Oct. 22, 1844, was based on a long line of doubtful chronological figures extending back over twenty-three hundred years. They were disputed by able scholars. Now, what did that uneducated girl know about these ancient chronological dates? Absolutely nothing. She simply believed Miller's strong, positive statements without knowing whether they were reliable or not.

The same was true of the great mass of those who accepted Miller's preaching. Very few, indeed, were persons with either education or ability. They were persons who could easily be moved by mere assertions and excitement. Of this there was plenty.

Ellen was so carried away with these positive assertions that for days she sat propped up in bed, working to earn a few pennies to buy Advent tracts to give away. (p. 38.) When able to be up, she went out warning her young friends. She says that "several entire nights were spent by me" in this way.

Then she gives an account of how different ones in exciting meetings would fall powerless to the floor. (p. 47.) The children were affected the same way. The Advent preachers experienced the same thing. (p. 49.)

For weeks before the day set, business was laid aside, and

exciting meetings constantly held. (p. 51.) All this, Ellen, with her parents, accepted without question as the power of God, the work of the Holy Ghost witnessing to the truth of what Miller taught. But was it? No. Candid people will see that it was simply their overwrought, excited feelings; that was all.

Their disappointment was great. Then followed confusion, divisions, and the wildest fanaticism–dreams, trances, visions, speaking with tongues, claims of prophetic gifts, and the like.

Elder White, in *Present Truth*, May, 1850, says: "J.V. Himes, at the Albany Conference in the spring of 1845, said that the seventh-month movement produced mesmerism seven feet deep." Elder Himes, next to Miller, was the strongest man in that work. When it was over, that was his estimate of the spirit that moved the people. And he was right.

It was inevitable that this would be the result with such a class of people expecting such an awful event on a definite day. Miller, Himes, Litch, and all the leaders in that work soon confessed it had been a mistake. But Elder White, Bates, Holt, Andrews, and Ellen Harmon (Mrs. White) all still held onto that work as correct–as the mighty power of God.

Their followers still defend it, and claim it was of God. Mrs. White, in all her visions and revelations, goes back to it over and over as the special providence of God, the power of the Holy Ghost. With her and with her people, it is like the coming out of Egypt, the crossing of the Red Sea, the pillar of fire by night, the cloud by day, the voice of God from Sinai, the foundation of the greatest message God ever sent to men, the last *test* of all ages!

But was this message from God? Most assuredly not. Abundant facts prove it. It was simply the work of fallible men misguided by zeal without knowledge.

In fixing the exact time and setting a definite day for Christ to come, they contradicted the plainest warnings Jesus ever gave, over and over. He said: "But of that day and hour knoweth no man, no, not the angels of heaven, but my Father only." (Matt. 24:36.)

"It is not for you to know the times or the seasons which the Father hath put in his own power." (Acts 1:7.)

All this was brushed aside. They did know the time and the day. Everybody who did not agree with them would be rejected of God and lost. And that spirit has followed their work more or less ever since.

They met what they richly deserved for so blindly disregarding the word of God. They were bitterly disappointed, and had to endure the mocking of those whom they had condemned to destruction for not agreeing with them. Now read the Lord's condemnation of such work. "When a prophet speaketh in the name of the Lord, if the thing follow not, nor come to pass, that is the thing which the Lord hath not spoken, but the prophet hath spoken it presumptuously; thou shalt not be afraid of him." (Deut. 18:22.)

This is exactly what the Adventists did in 1843, and then again in 1844. They spoke in the name of the Lord, and it did not come to pass. So do not fear them.

Seventh-day Adventists now condemn those who are at present trying to figure out the exact time when the Lord will come. Thus the *Advent Review*, March 2, 1916, says: "Satan would have us believe that we can actually figure out the proximity of the Lord's return; that by casting up figures and computing statistics we can determine how far the last gospel message has extended, and how nearly Israel is made up." Here the *Review* condemns exactly what Miller did in 1844. It says this is the work of Satan. Then, was it not his work back there?

In an article entitled "A False Prophet Exposed," published in their English paper, *Present Truth*, Feb. 4, 1915, they say: "Now if there is one characteristic above another that marks out a false prophet, it is the unscriptural practice of setting a definite time for the return of our Lord."

This was said in condemnation of "Pastor" C.T. Russell setting the time for the "end of the times of the Gentiles" to occur in 1914. But if it was wrong to set time for 1914, why was it not wrong to set it for 1844, sixty years before? If it was "unscriptural" in one case, why was it not in the other?

Although originating with this error, Seventh-day Adventists now condemn time-setting, as already stated. Referring to Christ's words in Matt. 24:36, Mark 13:33, and Acts 1:7, they say:

"In spite of these words, some have from time to time set dates for Christ's coming. Such date-setting leads often to fanaticism, and when the date passes, discouragement and utter skepticism are liable to possess the souls of the date-setters." (*Review and Herald*, June 7, 1917.)

Time and again this has been proven absolutely true. If one sentence had been added to this statement, it would have been complete, and that would have been this: "As an illustration of one of the worst instances of time-setting, see the time set by Adventists, Oct. 22, 1844, and the awful fanaticism and ruin that followed it."

If setting a definite time proves Mr. Russell and others false prophets, why does it not prove William Miller, Joseph Bates, and Mrs. White false prophets also? Seventh-day Adventists can not consistently condemn this practice in others without condemning themselves, for they, too, have been guilty of it, as we show in the chapter on "The Shut Door."

In December 1844, only two months after that failure, Mrs. White began having "visions." In the first one she says: "God has shown me in holy vision," etc. She looked for the Advent people, but could not see them. She was told to look higher. There, way up above the world, she saw them on a high path going to the city.

A glorious light was behind them. It was the Millerite warning of two months previous. Those who denied that work fell off the path down with "all the wicked world which God had rejected." (*Word to the Little Flock*, p. 14.)

To deny that God was in that 1844 time-setting work, was to be lost. Thus she says: "As the churches refused to receive the first angel's message [Miller's work], they rejected the light from heaven and fell from the favor of God." (*Early Writings*, p. 101.)

Trying to excuse their failure in 1843, she says: "I have seen that the 1843 chart was directed by the hand of the Lord, and that it should not be altered; that the figures were as the Lord wanted them; that his hand was over, and hid, a mistake in some of the figures." (*Early Writings*, p. 64.)

Here she has the presumption to throw upon almighty God

the responsibility for the blunder and failure in 1843. Is not this charging God with folly? And this to excuse their own folly.

Again she says: "The Advent movement of 1840-44 was a glorious manifestation of the power of God." (*The Great Controversy*, Vol. IV., p. 429.)

So God is made responsible for all their time-setting failures, both in 1843 and 1844.

Here the visions of this girl were added to the Advent movement of 1844. After this she had visions almost daily, every week or so at least. The Advent people generally regarded them as simply hallucinations of her own mind, caused by her feeble condition of body and the excitements around her. Some of her best friends so regarded them. Elder White himself, in *A Word to the Little Flock* (p. 22), published in 1847, quotes one of her friends who was familiar with her exercises.

This brother says: "I can not endorse sister Ellen's visions as of divine inspiration, as you and she think them to be; yet I do not suspect the least shade of dishonesty in either of you in this matter. I may, perhaps, express to you my belief in the matter without harm–it will, doubtless, result either in your good or mine. At the same time, I admit the possibility of my being mistaken. I think that what she and you regard as visions from the Lord, are only religious reveries, in which her imagination runs without control upon themes in which she is most deeply interested. While so absorbed in these reveries, she is lost to everything around her. Reveries are of two kinds, sinful and religious. Hers is the latter...Religion is her theme, and her reveries are religious. In either case, the *sentiments*, in the main, are obtained from previous teaching, or study. I do not by any means think that her visions are from the devil."

Elder Bates says that his first impressions of her visions were that they were only "what was produced by a protracted debilitated state of her body." (same work, p. 21.)

These statements exactly express the author's deliberate opinion of Mrs. White's so-called visions. After a thorough acquaintance with her for many years, I became satisfied that this was the true explanation of her supposed revelations. I have personally known other Seventh-day Adventist sisters who had visions similar to those of Mrs. White. All were most devout Christians, sincere beyond a question, but misguided and fanatical. Not being encouraged in their alleged "gifts," after awhile their visions ceased.

Since Mrs. White's death, a Seventh-day Adventist sister in Los Angeles, California has been having visions similar to Mrs. White's visions. She has quite a following who accept them of God. But the conference officials denounce them as spurious.

Another sister in Washington, D.C., has visions, and claims to be the successor of Mrs. White.

For quite a while Mrs. White herself doubted the genuineness of her own visions. She says: "I was sometimes tempted to doubt my own experience." (*Early Writings*, p. 18.) Then, years later, after she had had a long experience with her own visions, she says: "In the night I have awakened my husband, saying, 'I am afraid I shall become an infidel.'" (*Testimonies*, Vol. I., p. 597.)

Did any prophet of the Bible, any true prophet of God, ever talk like that? If she was really sure her visions were of God, there could have been no occasion for her fears that she would become an infidel. This confession shows that she was not herself certain that her visions were from God.

Notice here how she turns to her stronger-minded husband to help her out of her doubts. Had it not been for his consistent encouragement, she, like others, would, in all probability, have given up her visions.

That she suffered for years with a severe form of epilepsy is not generally known; but such is the case. See this subject treated in the chapter on "Philosophy of Her Visions."

In 1846 she married Elder White. He strongly encouraged her in these visions. Also in that year Elder Joseph Bates endorsed them. Thus encouraged, her doubts as to their source seem to have been relieved. That she was more or less sincere in this misconception and deception seems evident from the general tenor of her life. A careful study of her writings shows that each year she became a little stronger in her claims of inspiration, till finally she made the assertion that all her utterances, even in a letter, were inspired. For a further explanation of her visions see the chapter just referred to.

The foundation of Adventism was laid in 1844. The visions of Mrs. White were added to this late in the same year. Then, in 1846, the Sabbath was added. Next came the sanctuary. Then the three messages. Later, the health reform, short dress, and other matters.

All these were, from time to time, simply added to, and built upon, the original time-setting foundation of 1844. Hence, all Seventh-day Adventists point back to this as the great event in their history.

After their marriage, Mrs. and Mrs. White visited believers in all the New England states. These companies were small, scattered, and poor. Hence, both endured many privations for a time, and induced them to keep the Sabbath, though at first they saw no importance in it. He accepted Mrs. White's visions, and she accepted his Sabbath-keeping.

She soon accepted all his theories about the Sabbath; that it was the seal of God, the great test of Christianity, and that it must be kept from 6 PM to 6 PM, instead of from sunset to sunset, as they now keep it.

Right after this she went to heaven, and Jesus took her into the Most Holy, lifted the lid of the ark, and showed her the tables of stone with the Sabbath shining above all the rest of the Commandments (*Early Writings*, p. 26.)

Query: Why did not Jesus tell her she was breaking the Sabbath every week by beginning it at the wrong time?

Her first child was born in August, 1847. They occupied a part of a brother's house, and rented furniture. Elder White worked hauling stone to the railroad; then cut wood for fifty cents a day (*Testimonies for the Church*, Vol. I., p. 82.)

By this it will be seen that he was not a man of influence among the Adventists. His wife's visions were generally discredited.

In 1848 they visited different places in New England. They also went to western New York, where they met a few Adventists.

In 1849, Elder White began publishing his first paper, *Present Truth*. Some numbers were printed in one place, and some in another, for two years.

In 1850, at Paris, Maine, he issued the first number of the *Review and Herald*.

In 1852 they moved to Rochester, N.Y. Here he started a small printing office.

In 1853 they came as far west as Michigan, where they found scattered brethren; then visited Wisconsin.

JAMES WHITE

In 1855 they moved their office to Battle Creek, Mich. This remained the headquarters of the denomination for about fifty years. Gradually large interests were built up here, a great printing plant, the large Sanitarium, the College, the Tabernacle, etc. These were the days of greatest harmony and material prosperity. These were the days when I was most prominent with them, and helped in building all these institutions.

Finally Dr. Kellogg and Mrs. White parted company, and he, with the Sanitarium, was separated from the denomination. Then the headquarters were moved to Washington, D.C., in 1903.

BRIEF SKETCH OF HER LIFE

After locating in Battle Creek in 1855, for the next twenty-five years Mrs. White traveled and labored, either with her husband or with some efficient help, in many of the states from Maine to California. Her influence with her people had now become settled and supreme. No one dared question her authority or inspiration. About every year, men of more or less prominence withdrew on account of disbelief in her "testimonies," as they now call them. But the great majority remained loyal to her.

In August, 1881, her husband died. This was really a blessing to her. He had largely lost his influence with the church, and others were in the high offices. She began to be influenced more by them than by him.

This worried him. He tried to get me to go with him and break their influence over her. He wrote me that we two would go on the General Conference Committee and so get them out of office, and break their growing influence over her. Here is his letter to me about two months before he died: Battle Creek, May 24 [1881].

> Bro. Canright:
>
> The *Review* will tell of our plans. We shall depend on you to help us...We hope you can join us in our labors. There will be efforts made to get you to Wisconsin, to have you go here and there...I hope we shall see our way out and be able to labor in union...Elders Butler and Haskell have had an influence over her that I hope to see broken. It has nearly ruined her. These men must not be supported by our people to do as they have done...It is time there was a change in the officers of the General Conference. I trust that if we are true and faithful, the Lord will be pleased that we should constitute two of that board.
>
> (Signed) James White.

About this same time Elder White is said to have remarked to Elder Butler: "You and Haskell have warped my wife's mind, and I am going home to take the warp out of it."

When we were together he went over more full the plans referred to in his letter. But August 6 he suddenly died. His words bring out clearly the fact that he knew his wife was influenced, in her visions, by others. All his life he had done that himself. As these two men were opposed to him, he feared their influence over her, if with them, as they and she had planned. So he urged me to go with him and his wife to make a strong team, and so keep her with himself and away from them. This is the way matters stood when he died.

A few days later Elder Butler told me that Elder White's death was providential to save the church from a split. This left Butler strongly in the lead for several years more. Finally he and Mrs. White fell out, and he retired to a little farm in Florida, and was silent for many years.

He told her she could go her way, and he could go his. It was generally reported that he had lost confidence in the "testimonies." The fact that he quit the work for so long a time indicated it. She had given him a severe "testimony" which he did not like.

Elder White was not a literary man, not a student of books, not scholarly, not a theologian. He understood neither Hebrew, Greek, nor Latin, read only the common English version of the Bible, and seldom ever consulted translations.

He was a business man, had a large business ability, and was a born leader of men. His study and work were largely devoted to building up large business institutions, such as publishing houses, the Sanitarium, the college, general and state conferences, and to finance. Here he made a success.

But his literary attainments were meager indeed. Compared with the great reformers like Luther, Melancthon, Wesley, and others, he was a complete failure. He attended high school only twenty-nine weeks, and learned enough simply to teach a country school.

Though he published and edited papers for thirty years, he produced no commentary, no critical work, no book on any doctrinal subject. He published two bound books: *Life Sketches*, a simple story of his and his wife's lives, and *Life of Miller*, taken almost wholly from another author.

He drew his knowledge from observation and from conversing with leading men who were students. All doctrinal subjects requiring study he turned over to these men for them to dig out, after which he used them himself.

Neither he nor his wife ever originated a single doctrine held by the Seventh-day Adventists. The doctrine of the second advent they received from Miller; and all the prophetic dates they accepted from him exactly as arranged.

The Sabbath they took from Bates, together with his unscriptural 6 PM time to begin and end it. Then they followed J.N. Andrews in changing to sunset time.

The theory of the sanctuary in heaven they accepted from Elder O.R.L. Crosier, who afterwards repudiated it.

Later they accepted from Andrews the theory of the three messages and the two-horned beast, as applied to the United States.

The sleep of the dead they got from the First-day Adventists, with whom they soon fell out and had many bitter controversies.

From the writer they accepted three items of vital importance to their financial success. Early in the work Elder White arranged what was called "Systematic Benevolence." Every person was asked to put down in a book a statement of all his property at its full value, and pay so much on each dollar, whether the property was producing anything or not.

All were asked to pledge ahead each year what they would give each week. This is not tithing. No one can tell a year ahead what he may have, nor whether he may live that long. This plan was strongly endorsed by Mrs. White in the first volume of her "Testimonies to the Church." She says: "The plan of Systematic Benevolence is pleasing to God...God is leading his people in the plan of Systematic Benevolence." (pp. 190, 191.)

"Systematic Benevolence looks to you as needless; you overlook the fact that it originated with God, whose wisdom is unerring. This plan he ordained." (p. 545.)

So, God ordained this plan! It ought to have worked then, but it failed. This is confessed in their *Lake Union Herald* of Feb. 24, 1915, thus: "The money was called Systematic Benevolence, but the method did not prove satisfactory, and it was discontinued with us after two years' trial, and tithing according to the income of the individual was adopted in its stead."

Yes, and I was the one who made that change.

In the winter of 1875-6, Elder White requested me to visit all the churches in Michigan and straighten up their finances, which were in bad shape. I found them discouraged, and behind on their pledges, and dissatisfied with the Systematic Benevolence plan.

After studying the subject, I set that plan all aside, and had the churches adopt the plan of tithing as practiced by that church ever since. All were pleased, and the finances greatly improved.

I went to Battle Creek and laid the new plan before Elder White. He readily accepted it, and the change was made general. Now, was the other plan ordained by God? Was he pleased with it? And did he direct Mrs. White to say so? No; her husband got it up, and she endorsed it. That was all.

After this, she just as strongly endorsed the tithing as I arranged it. Was my plan better than the Lord's? This is a fair sample of how Mrs. White endorsed what others studied out, but had no special light on, herself, as she professed to have.

At the same time, I found the churches neglecting the Lord's Supper, in many cases for years at a time, nor was there any regular time for business meetings. So I induced all the churches where I went to adopt the plan of holding regular quarterly meetings, four times yearly, for all business matters. This, also, was adopted, and has been practiced by the denomination ever since.

Up till 1877, no money for any purpose, not even for Sabbath schools, was collected in their churches on the Sabbath. It was regarded as sacrilegious to take money on the Sabbath. But at Danvers, Mass., I disregarded this custom, and took the first collection on the Sabbath, Aug. 18, 1877.

It worked well. I went to Battle Creek, and laid the matter before Elder White and his wife, who readily approved of it. It has been universally adopted by the denomination ever since, and has brought hundreds of thousands of dollars into their treasury.

This again illustrates how Mrs. White simply followed after

BRIEF SKETCH OF HER LIFE

and endorsed what others studied out. Thus, the *Review and Herald*, Sept. 7, 1916, says: "These extracts will clearly show [Mrs. White] to be very helpful in confirming the believers in the conclusions they had reached from the study of the Scriptures."

Exactly. Mrs. White simply followed after and "confirmed" what others had studied out, and that was all she ever did do.

In the *Lake Union Herald*, Nov. 1, 1916, is given another good proof of this. It tells how one brother (Wayne), ten years previous, and on for several years, worked up the plan to get missionary funds by selling what they now call "Harvest Ingathering" papers. It has proved a great success.

It is now one of their established plans of raising money. After Mr. Wayne had worked this up to a success, Mrs. White came forward and endorsed it. The paper says: "Shortly after the plan was started, Sister White wrote Brother Wayne of the light God had given her concerning this plan, fully endorsing it as being in harmony with the mind of the Lord."

Here it is again, the same old story. Some one studies out a successful plan, then Mrs. White has a revelation concerning it. With her, the Lord was always behind in his instructions!

By far the most important part of their work is the circulation of their publications. In *Testimonies*, Vol. IX., p. 65, Mrs. White says, "In the night of March 2, 1907, many things were revealed to me regarding the value of our publications," and the small effort being made to circulate them.

What occasioned this revelation? On the same page she says: "The afternoon of March 2 I spent in counsel with Brother and Sister S.N. Haskell." Then followed two pages telling of the burden Haskell had on this subject, and his plans to push the work. Haskell had filled her mind with his ideas and plans, and then the night following she is restless in her sleep, and has a "revelation" strongly endorsing Haskell's plans.

So it always was from first to last. This is where her revelations have been of great service to the church. Indeed, they claim that it could not have succeeded without her "testimonies." Leading men went ahead and studied out doctrines and plans, then she followed with a "divine revelation," endorsing each of these in turn. That gave each a divine sanction.

They can not name a single move that has not come that way. Take their Tract and Missionary Society. Elder Haskell first started this. Then Mrs. White took it up and endorsed it.

S.N. HASKELL

Doctor Kellogg strongly advocated the medical missionary work. Mrs. White then followed with a strong endorsement of that. So it has been with every move made.

These illustrations demonstrate the fact that she has been led by men, not by God, in her testimonies. Now the leaders turn this squarely around and say that she has led in all the moves made, which is absolutely false. They do this to exalt her testimonies so they can use them to carry out their plans.

Never in the history, from Adam till now, had God ever chosen an uneducated man or woman as a leader in any crisis or reformation of the church. "Moses was learned in all the wisdom of the Egyptians, and was mighty in words and deed." (Acts 7:22.) Ezra "was a ready scribe in the law of Moses." (Ezra 7:6.) He was a trusted friend of the king. Nehemiah was cupbearer to the king, and in high authority (Neh. 2:1.) To Paul, Agrippa said, "Much learning doth make thee mad." (Acts 26:24.)

The Christian church owes more to Paul than to all the other apostles combined. He was the great, educated leader of the infant church. In the great Reformation at the birth of Protestantism, all the reformers were among the great scholars of that age, men who had mighty influence with the rulers and the masses. Such were Luther, Melancthon, Erasmus, Zwingle, Knox and many others.

John Wesley, the great English reformer, the father of Methodism, was of a royal family, a graduate of Oxford, London, the highest seat of learning in the English world. He was a man of immense influence, and was a ripe scholar. His prose works comprise seven volumes, besides numerous hymns, *Notes on the New Testament*, etc.

Mrs. White had none of the earmarks of a great reformer. Her books of any general interest are easily shown to have been copied largely from other authors, and polished up by her assistants. See the chapter dealing with her plagiarisms.

She never had the slightest influence with rulers or with the public generally, as all other reformers from Moses to Wesley had. She has instilled into her people a spirit so intensely sectarian, and hostile to all other churches, that both in the homeland and mission fields, they are regarded as hindrances to Christian work.

After over seventy years' trial, Mrs. White is regarded by all the Christian world as a false teacher, and this by the most intelligent, devout and earnest Christian workers of this generation.

Mr. Moody, an earnest advocate of the doctrine of Christ's second coming, condemned their whole movement. There must be some good reasons for all this.

The year 1846 marked the turning point in her life. August 30 of that year she married Elder James White, an 1844 Adventist. He was six years older than she, well and strong, and better educated. She was a sickly girl of only nineteen, absolutely penniless.

Later years proved that Elder White was a shrewd, far-seeing business man, with a strong, dominating will, a born leader. In a work entitled *The Vision of Mrs. White* (pp. 25, 26), E.P. Woodward, of Portland, Maine, gives the following estimate of the relative mental strength of Mr. and Mrs. White: "Behold this impressible girl, religious to an extreme, her nerves weakened and shattered by the circumstances of her childhood, just passing through her first great physiological and psychological change in her life, thrown into close contact with this dominant mind–and that at a time when the very air was surcharged with religious excitement, aggravated by bitter and hopeless disappointment."

What influence this strong, masterful mind would naturally have over that frail girl is easy to see. In later years, one needed to be in the family but a short time to see that his will was supreme, and that she constantly had to bow to it. I have often heard him speak to her sharply, while she made no defense.

Elder J.N. Andrews told me that he once sat by while Mrs. White read a mild testimony of reproof to her husband. He said, "Ellen, hand me that." She obeyed, and he took it and threw it into the fire! Elder White, however, could readily see that it would be greatly to his advantage to have divine endorsement for all his plans; hence, from the very first, he strongly sustained her visions; would never tolerate in others the slightest question as to their genuineness, although he himself had little respect for them when they reproved him.

In the first publication he issued, *A Word to the Little Flock* (1847, p. 13), he argued for visions in the last days. Hence, from the first, Mrs. White had the influence and encouragement of her husband to believe her visions were of God. This helped her own wavering faith.

In the same year (1846), Elder Bates endorsed her visions. He was a man of far more influence than Elder White or his wife. He himself was a dreamer, a visionary, trusting in dreams and visions. He says: "I asked for a dream, visions, or any way that was consistent with His will to instruct me. The next thing, as near as I can now recollect, was the following dream." (*Past and Present Experience,* p. 75; 1848.)

Being a visionary himself, he readily endorsed the visions of Mrs. White. He was the first man of any influence to do so. This greatly encouraged Mrs. White, and increased her influence.

At the same time Elder Bates pressed on Mrs. White and her husband the necessity of keeping the Sabbath. Though they at first attached no importance to it, yet they accepted it.

Mrs. White herself has given an illustration of how her testimonies were given to order as requested by officials needing them. In 1867 the first building for the Health Reform Institute (Sanitarium) was being planned and built at Battle Creek, Mich. Elder White was sick and away from home. So Elder Loughborough and others went ahead with the work.

HEALTH INSTITUTE 1866

Money was needed. As usual, they went to Mrs. White and asked for a testimony to the brethren to donate the means. This was delivered as ordered. Here are a few lines from it: "Here, I was shown, was a worthy enterprise for God's people to engage in." "Our people should have an institution of their own." "Especially should those who have means invest in this enterprise." (*Testimonies for the Church,* Vol. I., pp. 492, 494.)

She goes on through several pages urging the brethren to send in their means to erect that building. Over and over she says, "I was shown" this–a clear, inspired revelation from God. So means came in. I myself gave twenty-five dollars, and have the certificate now.

The building was begun, and the first story up, when Elder White returned. He was angry because he had not planned and bossed it. It had all to come down--every stone. Then he put it all up again another way at a loss of $11,000 of the Lord's money!

This put Mrs. White in a bad fix. He demanded another testimony repudiating the first one. She had to humbly obey, and did. Here is her confession: "What appeared in *Testimony No. 11* concerning the Health Institute should not have been given until I was able to write out all I had seen in regard to it...They [the officials at Battle Creek] therefore wrote to me that the influence of my testimony in regard to the institute was needed immediately to move the brethren upon the subject. Under these circumstances I yielded my judgment to that of others, and wrote what appeared in No. 11 in regard to the Health Institute...In this I did wrong" (Id., p. 563.)

This proves that Mrs. White was influenced by the officials to write a testimony, just as they wanted it, to use to get money. Then, at Elder White's demand, she writes another testimony, confessing that the first one was wrong! Did the Lord give her that testimony? Did he do wrong? How was she "shown" what she says she "saw"?

SANITARIUM 1877

Here see the controlling influence her husband had over her. She reversed herself to suit his desire to rule in all things. Referring to this transaction, Dr. J.H. Kellogg, in his reply to an examining committee, said: "It was an infamous thing, a crime, tearing that thing down, for no other reason than because James

White was not consulted." But through her testimonies Mrs. White gave divine sanction to it all.

After the death of her husband in 1881, Mrs. White labored extensively in Europe in company with several leading men. Here she visited England, Germany, France, Switzerland, Italy, and the Netherlands while their work there was yet young. Her influence in giving divine endorsements to the work helped to impart zeal to the workers.

She remained there two years. Returning to America, she labored here as usual till 1891, when she went to Australia. She remained there for nine years, visiting the different colonies, and encouraging and imparting zeal to the workers there.

She also did much writing while there. There, also, her "divine authority" was of great value in endorsing the plans and operations of the workers.

In 1900, at the age of seventy-three, she returned to the United States, still full of vigor. During 1901, she made a trip through the Southern states, visiting the places where the work had been started. She attended the General Conference also that year.

About this time there was a great rebellion and rupture in the work at headquarters in Battle Creek, Much., where their largest and most important institutions were located. Dr. J.H. Kellogg, head of their Sanitarium there, was a man of influence, having many friends.

Mrs. White tried to rule him as she had ruled so many others, but he was too strong for her so she denounced him in unsparing terms. The result was that the Sanitarium, with a large number of influential men, went out of the denomination.

BATTLE CREEK PUBLISHING OFFICE

Then Mrs. White demanded that the headquarters of the denomination should be removed from that rebellious city. In 1902 the Sanitarium and their large publishing house at Battle Creek were burned down, whether accidentally, providentially, or, well, some other way, was an open question.

At first Mrs. White styled these fires mysterious, and forbade any one attempting to explain them. In a testimony dated Feb. 20, 1902, soon after the burning of the Sanitarium, she said: "Let no one attempt to say why this calamity was permitted to come...Let no one try to explain this mysterious providence." But later, in 1903, she called these fires "judgments," and reproved the brethren for not having tried to find out their meaning. She said: "In the calamities that have befallen our institutions in Battle Creek, we have had an admonition form God. Let us not pass this admonition carelessly by without trying to understand its meaning." "God would not have let the fire go through our institutions in Battle Creek without a reason. Are you going to pass by the providence of God without finding out what it means? God wants us to study into this matter." (*Special Testimonies,* Series B, No. 6, pp. 6, 11, 33.)

In 1905, their next largest publishing house, located at Mountain View, Cal., fifty-five miles south of San Francisco, was destroyed by the earthquake of that year. A new building was erected. But the next year this was also destroyed by fire. In this fire, Mrs. White herself was the heaviest personal loser. Illustrations for which she paid a New York artist thousands of dollars, to reillustrate some of her larger books, had carelessly been left out of the vault and were completely destroyed. After this, Mrs. White had little to say about these fires being "judgments" from God. The lightning had struck too close to her this time.

April 24, 1911, their publishing house at their new headquarters in Washington, D.C., had a $28,000 fire. Wherever they have gone, fires seem to have followed them.

After the rebuilding of the Battle Creek Sanitarium, the leading officials, backed by Mrs. White, tried to loosen Dr. Kellogg's hold on it and bring it under ecclesiastical control. She said: "Our leading brethren, the men in official positions, are to examine the standing of the Battle Creek Sanitarium, to see whether the God of heaven can take control of it." (*Testimonies,* Series B, No. 6, p. 33.)

But the leading brethren decided that God couldn't take control of it, and so threw it overboard. Then Mrs. White predicted more judgments on the doomed city, none of which have come.

SANITARIUM 1884

Backed by her testimonies, the officials then undertook a determined campaign to crush Dr. Kellogg. In a council meeting, Elder A.G. Daniells, president of their General Conference, said: "Dr. Kellogg has an imperious will which needs to be broken."

This reveals the spirit which actuated both her and them. If they could not rule, they were ready to crush men, break their wills, and call judgments down on them. But in this case their efforts failed. They simply lost Dr. Kellogg, their most capable and noted physician, and their largest and best equipped sanitarium, which Dr. Kellogg's genius and untiring efforts had built up.

For several years Mrs. White remained largely in California, visiting the work in different places, but spent much time in writing. In 1905 she attended the General Conference in Washington, D.C. After this she returned to California. Here she wrote as follows: "While at Loma Linda, Cal., Apr. 16, 1906, there passed before me a most wonderful representation." (*Life Sketches of Mrs. E.G. White*, p. 407, edition 1915.)

She stood on an eminence with an angel by her side. She saw great buildings fall, saw awful destruction, and heard the cry of the dying. "The destroying angels of God were at work," she said. Two days later (April 18), San Francisco was visited with a great earthquake, just as she had seen! But when did she relate this great warning? Not until days after the city had fallen!

On page 409, same book, she says: "It has taken me many days to write out a portion of what was revealed those two nights." Notice: she did not tell what the angel showed her till after the event had occurred. Why did not the angel tell her what city and when? Why did she not tell it the next day? Evidently that "vision of the night" was an afterthought, when it was safe to tell it. But it "went" with her followers.

After the failures of the first few years, she was cautious about naming dates or places till after the events had occurred.

This earthquake, so near, frightened her. So she immediately wrote: "Out of the cities, out of the cities, this is the message the Lord has been giving me." (same page.)

In 1909, Mrs. White again visited Washington, where she attended the General Conference and took an active part, though eighty-one years old. On her return to California she attended meetings in various places, speaking as usual. During the remaining six years of her life she was too feeble to travel; so she spent the time in writing books, with the aid of her helpers.

It is known that for many years the greater portion of the material for her larger and most important books was gathered, arranged, and written out, not by Mrs. White herself, but by her assistants. She simply supervised it.

Her biographer confesses this. He says: "She found time to supervise the revision of *Sketches from the Life of Paul.*" (p. 434, same book quoted above.) Largely, therefore, these books were the production of others, "supervised" by her.

Were these helpers inspired also? These books are now accepted by her followers as infallibly correct, all inspired of God!

We are informed by her near relatives that during these closing years of her life, when these important books were being prepared, she often did not know her nearest friends, nor even some of her attendants whom she saw almost daily. When she attempted to speak in her home church, she repeated herself over and over again, and had to be told when to stop. None of these weaknesses appear in the composition of her works prepared at that time, because, like most of her earlier work, they were prepared by others. Surely her "supervision" could not have amounted to much in her mental condition at this time.

Finally she met with a fatal accident, a fall in her own home, Feb. 13, 1915, which resulted in her death July 16, 1915, at the age of nearly eighty-eight. Since her death the leaders have been exalting her and her "testimonies" more highly than before. They have been urging all their members to purchase a complete set of her works.

On the last page of one of their Sabbath school quarterlies for 1915 they say: "The complete writings of Mrs. E. G. White can now be obtained for a sum that brings them within the reach of practically every household." And the modest sum asked for a set of them is, in cloth, $18.60; in leather, $26.00–many times the price of a good morocco Bible.

And what has been the general effect of her "testimonies"? They have had a tendency to create in her followers a spirit of spying, faultfinding, criticizing, and judging one another. They have begotten in practically all the members, also, a narrow, bigoted, hostile spirit towards all other churches, which will not allow them to cooperate with other Christians in any evangelical work.

Indeed, they use every possible means to proselyte from all. With them all other churches are "Babylon," fallen because they refused to endorse Millerism. In *Early Writings* (*Supplement*, p. 37), Mrs. White says: "I saw that neither young nor old should attend their meetings." Little wonder her followers are narrow, bigoted, and exclusive.

In her obituary in the *Review and Herald*, Aug. 5, 1915, published soon after her death, Elder M.C. Wilcox said: "Her heart had large charity for those of the great Protestant denominations who could not see all that she saw." The quotation just given disproves this, and her views on the "shut door," which she held for years, ruled "the great Protestant denominations" out from God's mercy entirely.

To the last she applied the term "the fall of Babylon" to them. All her life energies were devoted to building up a sect, and promulgating narrow, sectarian views. She built high the middle wall or partition separating her followers from all other believers in Christ.

She was self-centered, and, on occasion, boastful. Her writings to her people abound in references to herself, to her ill health, and how she was often raised from beds of sickness to attend meetings. The evident object in this was to arouse sympathy, and to cause her followers to regard her as a special subject of God's providence.

As to boastful claims, the following is a sample: "I could prove greater devotion than any one living, engaged in the work." (*Testimonies*, Vol. I., p. 581.) (See Prov. 27:2.)

In advocating reforms, being naturally fanatical, she was inclined to take extreme views, which, although represented at the time as founded on divine revelations, she was later obliged to abandon or greatly modify.

With her friends she was sociable and an agreeable companion. But she would never tolerate any question of her authority, or any expressed doubt of her inspiration. Either would instantly stir her utmost wrath.

She admits tampering with the messages she says God gave her for others, and never seems certain that she wrote them just right. At first she says: "When obliged to declare the message, I would often soften them down, and make them appear as favorable for the individual as I could...It was hard to relate the plain, cutting testimonies given me of God." (*Testimonies,* Vol. I., p. 73.)

In *Testimonies,* Vol. V., p. 19, she denies having done this. She says: "I take back nothing. I soften nothing to suit their ideas, or to excuse their defects of character."

Later on, when she became more bold and severe in her work, she says that God would have "approved" had she "taken stronger ground and been much more severe." (Vol. I., p. 318.)

But finally, in 1901, she says: "I have written some very straight things...It may be that I have written too strong." (*A Response,* by Dr. Charles E. Stewart, p. 54.)

When, then, did she ever write right? And what shall be said of a prophet that would dare to tamper with God's messages? Upon her own, showing also that she was inclined to be cutting and severe.

In his comments on her life, Elder Wilcox further said: "Mrs. White sought to teach men to look to God for guidance in perplexity, and not to her or any other human being." This is far from true. She taught her own people to look to her constantly for guidance and instruction in every move and every detail of life. This could hardly be otherwise, when she claimed divine inspiration for all her writings, and that she was God's special "messenger" for this age.

Again, Elder Wilcox said: "Mrs. White never claimed or assumed leadership among this people." The very opposite is true. She did both. The highest officials in the denomination were subject to her. Like the Pope of Rome in medieval times, her power and influence in the church grew until she became supreme. She made and unmade conference presidents with a word of mouth or a stroke of the pen. She said who was and who was not to fill office. She said where to buy and build, and where not to. If she said, "Go ahead," no one in the whole denomination dared say otherwise, even though it meant the loss of thousands and tens of thousands of dollars.

The same writer further said that her testimonies were not "clubs to mangle, nor daggers to destroy souls." This is likewise false, for many of them were called for, written, and used in this very way.

As the reader peruses the succeeding chapters of this book, they will many times be impressed with these dominant characteristics of her life, mingled, as they were, with unbounded zeal and an intense religious nature.

Finally, in 1911, only four years before her death, as already stated, the claim of infallibility was set up for Mrs. White and her writings. This was but the logical climax to the claims which had already been made for her, and which she herself had made. Very appropriately the publication making this claim was written to silence heretics and apostates from the faith.

No greater claim was ever made for the Pope of Rome. As the claim of Papal infallibility was made late in the history of the Catholic Church, so the similar claim for Mrs. White came late in her life; and one is no more presumptuous than the other. So far as known, she never repudiated the claim, to the day of her death. Her son, Elder W.C. White, endorsed it.

But intelligent, thinking persons found that Mrs. White made mistakes; that she was often, very often, influenced by one person against another; and that she got her information from men, not God. The cases were so plain and so numerous that there could be no doubt about it. Then these persons must either acquiesce in what they doubted or disbelieved, or rebel and leave the denomination. Hence, all along the years, many left while others swallowed their doubts and remained.

We could fill pages of this book with simply the names of ministers, editors, teachers, physicians and missionaries who have left the church on account of disbelief in the inspiration of Mrs. White's writings. As to lay members, their number is legion, and rapidly increasing. Whole churches, and many of them, have left.

The worst feature of it is that many who once had implicit faith in Mrs. White, and then lost it, with that, lost faith in religion altogether. This is one of the sad but inevitable results of cults founded on such fanaticisms. This is why so many infidels are found in countries once so strongly Catholic. Having lost faith in the Pope and the church which claimed to have the only means of salvation, not knowing where else to turn and place their faith and trust, they gave up all. The same tendency to infidelity is seen in Utah among doubting Mormons. So, in this case, ex-Adventist infidels are found in large numbers wherever Seventh-day Adventists have worked. Battle Creek, so long the home of Mrs. White, is a terrible example of this.

There is now coming to be a strong influence to attract and hold thousands to the faith, by the official and financial opportunities offered, and this to persons of very ordinary ability and little training. These desirable positions blind the eyes and smother the conscience so that the obvious failures and mistakes of Mrs. White are passed over by dwelling on other things of which they feel sure.

The following pages of this book point out in detail, and by proofs indisputable, some of the most glaring of these mistakes and failures which the denominational leaders have done their utmost to hide from the public and to keep from their own people.

Notwithstanding all these mistakes and failures, Seventh-day Adventists claim that Mrs. White was equal to the greatest prophet God ever sent to men. But if she was inferior to none of the prophets of past ages, why did not God give her some credentials as he did them? She never wrought a single miracle; never claimed to, dared not claim it.

The prophets of old wrought many miracles. If the power of God was with her, why was there not some tangible proof of it? According to her own testimony, she had to be healed over and over often; but she had no power to heal others. Her oldest son, Henry, a strong, healthy boy of sixteen, was suddenly taken sick. She and her husband prayed over him earnestly but he died. Her last child was taken sick, and in a short time died. Her husband caught cold, became sick, was prayed for by herself, but suddenly died at the early age of sixty-one. She prayed over others who died. She never had any more power to heal the sick than any common Christian.

Where Now is Their "Spirit of Prophecy"?

From the beginning of their history, Seventh-day Adventists have claimed that they were the remnant church of Rev. 12:17 because they had a prophet among them; namely, Mrs. E.G. White. They have always insisted that they had the "spirit of prophecy" (Rev. 19:10.) When those opposed to their views have contended that we have the "spirit of prophecy" in the writings of the prophets as recorded in the Holy Scriptures, they have denied it, and have, in the most dogmatic fashion, contended that to have the spirit of prophecy there must be a living prophet in the church.

But now their prophet is dead. Where is their "spirit of prophecy" now? According to the long-used argument, they now have no spirit of prophecy, and therefore can not be the remnant church of Rev. 12:17. The death of Mrs. White killed their argument.

If they now say that they have the spirit of prophecy in her writings, they admit what they have always denied; namely, that the writings of the prophets contain the spirit of prophecy. If they have the spirit of prophecy in the writings left by their prophet, then we have always had the spirit of prophecy in the writings left by the prophets of the Bible.

All who have the Bible, and believe in that, have the spirit of prophecy contained in its writings. Therefore, the claim made by Seventh-day Adventists that they are the only body of Christians who have the spirit of prophecy is proven false by their own admission. Their former theory of the spirit of prophecy

WHERE NOW IS THEIR "SPIRIT OF PROPHECY?"

would compel them to bring forth immediately another living prophet, or surrender their argument in defense of the "spirit of prophecy" as represented in Mrs. White. This would destroy their whole theory on this subject.

For a period of seventy years they have claimed to be the remnant church of Rev. 12:17, because they had a living prophet in the church. But now their prophet is dead, and they have none any longer, whereby to prolong the "spirit of prophecy." They are now in the same condition as the other churches, and, according to their own argument, cannot now be the remnant church.

Upon the Scripture, "Where there is no vision, the people perish," their stock argument has been that, in order that the people shall be safe and surely guided, so that they shall not perish, there must be visions, and these the visions of a living prophet. Now the person is dead in whom alone they centered all true or proper visions. And now to them, where are the visions without which the people perish?

The author is indebted to Elder A.T. Jones, who was formerly the editor of their church paper, the *Review and Herald*, for the logical line or argument here presented. He rejected their narrow view on this subject, and was set aside without trial or hearing.

Up to the very last they were constantly appealing to Mrs. White for the settlement of new issues which kept arising among them. To the very close of her life, doctrinal disputes which were dividing the sympathies and allegiance of their leading men were all referred to her. As time goes on, who will now settle the new issues and questions constantly arising in their work? They will have to be settled by their uninspired, erring men, the same as in other churches. Hence they are just as liable to go wrong as are other churches.

Erroneous Views Concerning the Sanctuary

As the sanctuary plays so important a part in all of Mrs. White's visions, and in the Seventh-day Adventist faith generally, I will explain it briefly, without special argument.

Moses erected a building called the tabernacle, or sanctuary. It had two rooms. The first was called the Holy Place, the second, the Most Holy Place. In the first was the table of showbread, the candlestick, and the altar of incense; in the second, the ark. The two rooms were separated by "the veil." At the door of the first room was a curtain. Outside, in the court, stood the altar of burnt-offering.

In the court and in the Holy Place the priests ministered daily. No one entered the Most Holy Place except the high priest once a year, on the tenth day of the seventh month, the "day of atonement." (Lev. 23:37.) The services of this day were most important of all, and are fully described in Leviticus 16. On this day the high priest went into the Most Holy Place with the blood of a general offering for all the people, and made an atonement for all Israel. By sprinkling blood on and before the mercy seat on the ark, on the altar of incense, and on the altar of burnt-offering, he was said to "cleanse" the sanctuary from all the sins of the people.

All this was figurative and typical–an object lesson pointing to Christ.

Miller's time-setting views that Christ would come in 1844

were based on his calculations regarding the time for the "cleansing of the sanctuary." When the time passed, and Christ did not come, he, with all the leaders of the body of Adventists generally, soon acknowledged that he had been mistaken in the time. But a very few–Elder White, Ellen Harmon (Later Mrs. White), Elder Bates, and a few others–still held that the set day had been right. But they could not explain the failure.

About two years later, in 1846, one O.R.L. Crosier studied out the sanctuary subject very much as it is now held by Seventh-day Adventists. His view was accepted entirely by a few Adventists of that time, and Ellen Harmon (Mrs. White) shortly afterward had a "vision" in which she said the Lord showed her that the Crosier view was correct. She recommended its publication (see *A Word to the Little Flock*, pp. 11, 12.) The theory was that the earthly sanctuary was a type of one just like it up in heaven, and that this sanctuary in heaven, and that this sanctuary in heaven was the one referred to in Dan. 8:14, upon which was based the 1844 time-setting calculations; that Jesus, as our high priest, was to minister in the first room, or Holy Place, in heaven, from his ascension until Oct. 22, 1844, receiving there the confessed sins of believers, and that on Oct. 22, 1844, he finished his ministry in the Holy Place and went into the Most Holy, and there began the "cleansing of the sanctuary," which they said was also the anti-typical atonement. Notice that in this theory the atonement did not take place until over eighteen hundred years after Jesus died on the cross!

In Crosier's theory it was held that the work in the first apartment of the earthly sanctuary was for "forgiveness of sins" only; hence, when the work in the first apartment of the heavenly sanctuary closed (Oct. 22, 1844), there ended forgiveness of sins for all the world! Probation for sinners ended there! So, after 1844, Christ's work of atonement in the Most Holy Place was for saints only!

Mr. Crosier states that the object of this article on the sanctuary was to prove that probation ended in 1844, and Mrs. White endorsed it for that reason. (See the next chapter.) The Adventists knew nothing of this sanctuary theory until about two years after 1844. But when Crosier's theory was adopted, they linked up the "shut door" of the ten virgins parable, which they preached on in 1844, with what they now called the "shutting of the door" of the first room of the heavenly sanctuary when Jesus went into the second apartment.

It was not until 1849, five years after 1844, that they first invented the "open" door theory. (See next chapter.) But this "open door" was for saints only–the old Advent believers. This was the second step in the shut-door theory.

The Shut Door,
or, Probation for Sinners Ended Oct. 22, 1844

The above title indicates the theory held and dogmatically taught by all Seventh-day Adventists until the autumn of 1851. In later years they gradually modified it, and finally abandoned it altogether. Today they deny that they ever taught it at all!

But we shall see. All of their leaders advocated this unscriptural theory in the clearest possible terms until the time above indicated. Mrs. White had revelation after revelation in her visions during this same period, confirming this theory. Later, they were compelled either to reject her claims to inspiration, or deny that she ever taught such a theory.

The issue is plain. Here are the facts: The Seventh-day Adventist leaders of this early time were all in the great Millerite movement. In 1844 they staked all upon the assertion that the end of the world would come on Oct. 22, 1844. Of course, probation would end then.

To this time they applied the parable of the ten virgins recorded in Matt. 25:1-13. Just before giving this parable, Jesus had warned his disciples that his second advent would occur suddenly, when least expected. To enforce this teaching, he gave the parable. Ten virgins went out to meet the bridegroom. As he tarried longer than they expected, all fell asleep. When he did come, only five were ready to go with him to the wedding. These entered, and "the door was shut." Later the other five came and knocked, but they were too late to gain admittance.

The meaning is easy to understand. When Christ comes, all who are ready will be saved. The rest will be shut out, will be lost, for probation will be ended.

All the early Adventists, with Miller at their head, explained the parable in that way. And they were correct. When their set time passed they were dazed. They still insisted that their message had been right; probation had ended. They still hoped the Lord would come, and expected him any day. They ceased exhorting sinners, ceased praying for them, and said, "The door is shut."

This is the origin of the "shut door" theory. It then had with them no reference to any sanctuary, either on earth or in heaven. (Such an application was attempted later.) They had no "light" upon the sanctuary question till years after they had been preaching the "shut door."

It was not until five years later (1849) that Seventh-day Adventists invented the theory of an "open door" from Rev. 3:7, 8. This new position is stated by Mrs. White herself. She says: "The view of the 'open and shut door,' on pages 34-37, was given in 1849. The application of Rev. 3:7, 8 to the heavenly sanctuary and Christ's ministry was entirely new to me. I have never heard the idea advanced by any one." (*Supplement to Experience and Views*, p. 2.)

So she herself, with all the others, had for five years taught the "shut door" theory without any reference to an "open" door. Now they claim that they have taught both the "shut door" and the "open door" together from the first. Thus Elder Butler, referring to Rev. 3:7, 8, says: "Here was a door opened and a door shut." (*Replies to Canright,* p. 100.) He asserts that they taught both together from the beginning in 1844. Mrs. White's statement just quoted proves his statement to be false.

Here is a significant fact. After 1844, and on for over seven years, the term "shut door" occurs over and over in all the articles from the pens of all Seventh-day Adventists during that period - articles from Mrs. White, and Elders White, Holt, Arnold, Bates, and others. It is the center of their arguments. So prominent was this that they were called "Door Shutters." As such they were denounced by Mr. Miller and the other Adventists.

But after the shut-door theory was abandoned, that term

The Shut Door – Probation Ended Oct. 22, 1844

gradually disappears, until now for many years past it does not occur in their articles or publications at all. This fact alone proves that they have abandoned their theory of the shut door which they at first held, and which Mrs. White so strongly endorsed.

Seventh-day Adventists at first adopted the sanctuary theory to prove that the door of mercy was shut in 1844, a theory which Mrs. White and all of them held at that time. Here is my proof on this point:

> Ann Arbor, Mich.,
> Dec. 1, 1887
>
> Elder D.M. Canright:
>
> I kept the seventh day nearly a year, about 1848. In 1846 I explained the idea of the sanctuary in an article in an extra number of the *Day Star*, Cincinnati, O. The object of that article was to support the theory that the door of mercy was shut, a theory which I, and nearly all Adventists who had adopted William Miller's views, held from 1844 to 1848. Yes, I *know* that Ellen G. Harmon - now Mrs. White - held that shut-door theory at that time.
>
> Truly yours,
> O.R.L. Crosier

Now listen to Mrs. White: Topsham, Maine, Apr. 21, 1847. "...The Lord showed me in vision, more than one year ago, that Brother Crosier had the true light on the cleansing of the sanctuary, etc., and that it was his will that Bro. C. should write out the view which he gave us in the *Day Star* (extra), Feb. 7, 1846. I feel fully authorized by the Lord to recommend that extra to every saint." (*A Word to the Little Flock*, pp. 11, 12)

Here you have the origin and object of that sanctuary theory. All Adventists, including every branch under the leadership of Miller, for awhile after the day passed in 1844, held that probation for sinners had ended. Miller said: "We have done our work in warning sinners and in trying to awake a formal church. God in his providence has shut the door; we can only stir up one another to be patient." (*Advent Herald*, Dec. 11, 1844.)

Then, again, in the *Voice of Truth,* Feb. 19, 1845, he says: "I have not seen a genuine conversion since." Miller gave the keynote with which all agreed. But he, with all leading Adventists, very quickly gave up the theory, and ever after opposed it.

Elder G.I. Butler, in the *Review and Herald,* March 3, 1885, says: "As the time passed, there was a general feeling among the earnest believers that their work for the world was done...There can be no question that for months after the time passed it was the general sentiment that their work of warning the world was over...Their burden was gone, and they thought their work was done."

Yes, that was just what they did believe, probation was ended! Even Butler is compelled to admit it. Elder White admits the same thing to be true. He says: "In the absence of light in reference to the shut and open door of the heavenly sanctuary, the reader can hardly see how those who held fast their advent experience as illustrated by the parable of the ten virgins (Matt. 25:1-12), could fail to come to the conclusion that probation for sinners had ended." (*Life Sketches,* p. 121.)

But they did not have the "light," either on the sanctuary or the "open door," until years after 1844. This is equivalent to a confession that they believed probation for sinners had ended, and that they believed this for several years. Mrs. White adds her testimony to the foregoing, as follows: "After the passing of the time of expectation in 1844, Adventists still believed the Saviour's coming to be very near; they held that...the work of Christ as man's intercessor before God had ceased." (*Great Controversy,* edition 1884, p. 268.)

It is clear as light, from the admissions to be found in their own writings, that for a time after 1844 Seventh-day Adventists believed probation had ended.

ELDER JOSEPH BATES; HIS GREAT INFLUENCE UPON ELDER WHITE AND HIS WIFE

Elder Bates, New Bedford, Mass., was one of the most ardent coworkers with Miller and others in preaching the set time in 1844. He is reported to have spent $15,000 (all his fortune) in

THE SHUT DOOR – PROBATION ENDED OCT. 22, 1844

that work. He was highly regarded by the Adventists, with whom he had much influence. He was fairly well educated, a man of much force, and of very positive convictions. He met Elder White and his wife in the fall of 1846. He was then fifty-four years of age, in the prime of his life and influence.

JOSEPH BATES

Mrs. White was only nineteen, feeble, uneducated, unknown, save to a few, and these of no influence with Adventists. Elder White was only twenty-six, and had only a limited education. The part that he had taken in the 1844 work was so limited that he had little influence with the Adventists. He and his wife were penniless, absolutely poor. She was having "visions," which were generally regarded as the result of her poor health.

After a slight acquaintance, Bates endorsed her visions as of God, and threw all of his influence into supporting them. This was a wonderful advantage to Elder White and his wife. It was the turning point in their lives. They, therefore, readily accepted all of Bates' theories - the Sabbath, beginning it at 6 P.M. on Friday, and his argument that the day of atonement would last seven years from 1844, and end in the fall of 1851. With the Whites and others, he held strongly that probation for the world ended Oct. 22, 1844.

The pamphlet, *A Word to the Little Flock,* was published by Elder White in 1847. That he then believed that probation for sinners ended in 1844 is proved by his words on page 2, where he says: "From the ascension to the shutting of the door, October, 1844, Jesus stood with widespread arms of love and mercy; ready to receive, and plead the cause of every sinner who would come to God by him. On the tenth day of the seventh month, 1844, He passed into the Holy of Holies, where he has since been a merciful 'high priest over the house of God.' ...I think the following is a prophecy which has been fulfilling since October, 1844: 'And he saw that there was no man, and wondered that there was no intercessor.' (Isa. 59:14-16.)" Notice that after 1844 the sinner was left without an intercessor!

On page 21 of the little work is the following by Elder Bates: "Since the closing up of our work for the world, October, 1844." Their work for the world ended just there because there was no longer an "intercessor."

In the same little work, and between the two quotations already given, is the following from a vision by Mrs. White: "It was just as impossible for them [faithless Advent people] to get on the path again and go to the city, as all the wicked world which God had rejected." (p. 14.)

Carefully note how all the foregoing quotations agree: no intercessor for sinners after October, 1844; our work closed up for the world, October, 1844; all the wicked world which God had rejected! All three are so plain that no word of explanation is needed.

In 1850, Bates published a tract on the sanctuary. On page 9, he says: "The twenty-three hundred years are complete, ending in the fall of 1844...Here his [Christ's] work ceased ministering and mediating for the whole world forever...Here the door is shut." A study of this tract shows that Bates held that the day of atonement in the sanctuary in heaven began Oct. 22, 1844, and would last seven years, and, of course, end October, 1851. The

The Shut Door – Probation Ended Oct. 22, 1844

last six months, the gathering of the saints would occur.

He argued all this from the day of atonement as given in Leviticus 16. His argument was mere assumption, lacking proof. But it satisfied him. Elder White and his wife needed so much his influence, and besides, had so much confidence in his knowledge and ability, that they readily accepted his views and wrote in harmony with what he taught.

Here are the words of Elder Bates about that seven years: "The seven spots of blood on the Golden Altar and before the mercy seat, I fully believe, represent the duration of the judicial proceedings on the living saints in the Most Holy, all of which time they will be in their affliction, even seven years; God by his voice will deliver them, 'for it is the blood that maketh the atonement for the soul.' (Lev. 17:11.) Then the number seven will finish the day of atonement. (not redemption.) The last six months of this time, I understand, Jesus will be gathering in the harvest with his sickle, on the white cloud."

Again: "This is also where the door is shut–at the end of the twenty-three hundred days. The times of the Gentiles are over. Hos. 5:6, 7: 'They shall go with their flocks and their herds to seek the Lord; but they shall not find him; he hath withdrawn himself from them. Now shall a month devour them with their portions.' How evident that this is after the door is shut and Jesus had gone, or withdrawn himself, into the Holiest."

Again he says: "As soon as the day of atonement is ended, seven angels come out of the temple with the seven last plagues. (vs. 5, 6.) This is the duration of the third angel's message in Rev. 14:9-13." (*The Typical and Anti-typical Sanctuary*, pp. 10-13, 15, by Joseph Bates, 1850.)

Note that the times of the Gentiles were to end at the close of the twenty-three hundred days, in 1844–their probation ended there! Then the day of atonement would begin, and last seven years. This was to be the duration of the third angel's message–seven years.

This was Joseph Bates' theory. Jesus was to begin the atonement in heaven Oct. 22, 1844; it would continue seven years, and of course end in October, 1851. The last six months–May to October–would be the gathering of the saints.

It is plain from Mrs. White's writings of that time that she accepted and believed fully in this theory. Here is a "vision" given September, 1850, about one year before the seven years were to end: "Some are looking too far off for the coming of the Lord. Time has continued a few years longer than they expected, therefore they think it may continue a few years more...I saw that the time for Jesus to be in the Most Holy Place was nearly finished, and that time can not last but a little longer." (*Early Writings*, p. 58, ed. 1907.)

Jesus entered the Most Holy, it was claimed, Oct. 22, 1844. In September, 1850, he had been there six years. She at that time says she "saw" that his time to be there was nearly finished! See how exactly this agrees with the theory of Bates, published in the same year (1850)! These two were working together. Each knew what the other believed. Both wrote alike as to the time Jesus would be in the Most Holy Place. Bates said it would end in seven years–October, 1851, or only one year after he wrote. She said that Christ's time to be in the Most Holy Place was nearly finished when she wrote in 1850. Thus it would have been, if the theory Bates advanced had been correct.

One can easily see how she was blindly led by Bates. What she saw was not what God revealed to her, but what Bates taught her. Time has demonstrated that her "vision" was wrong. In 1850, when she wrote it, Jesus had been in the Most Holy Place, according to Advent teaching, only six years; yet she "saw" that his time to be there was nearly finished. But, instead of this being the case, nearly seventy long years have gone by, and, according to Seventh-day Adventist teaching, Jesus is still in the Most Holy Place in the sanctuary in heaven, and the day of probation for sinners has not yet ended! Any candid person will readily admit the error and the utter failure of that "vision."

But here is another "vision" still worse, written June 27, 1850: "My accompanying angel said, 'Time is almost finished. Get ready, get ready, get ready.'" A little further on she says: "Some of us have had time to get the truth, and to advance step by step, and every step we have taken has given us strength to take the next. But now time is almost finished...and what we have been years learning, they will have to learn in a few months." (*Early Writings*, pp. 64-67.)

In September, 1850, she limited the time to "a few months," "time almost finished," etc. Note how evidently she relied upon Bates' seven years. Had he been correct it would have been only a few months longer. It is clear that the deluded woman sincerely believed in Bates' ideas and interpretations or she never would have dared to write so dogmatically in her "vision" messages.

The passing of nearly seventy years has proved her "visions" to be, not a message from God, but the hallucinations of an overwrought mind, the result of her nervous condition. No holy angel ever told her what she claims he did; for he would have told her the truth. The study clearly reveals the fact that her "visions" were simply the product of her own mind, reflecting the views of those around her.

Miss Sarah B. Harmon, older sister of Mrs. White, in a letter written from Brookfield, N.Y., to Mrs. P.D. Lawrence, July 29 and 30, 1850, said: "I believe this is the last winter we shall see before Jesus, our great High Priest, comes out. Oh, let us live for God and sacrifice for him faithfully."* Here is additional evidence that Seventh-day Adventists had set the time for Christ to come in 1851.

EARLY ADVENTISTS TEACH THE SHUT DOOR

We now submit evidence from another important source of early Advent teaching; namely, *Present Truth*, published by Elder White in 1849 and 1850. In this publication several leading men gave their views of the "shut door" theory as held by all Seventh-day Adventists at that date. We quote first from Elder George W. Holt (*Present Truth*, December, 1849, p. 47.) He says: "Many will point us to one who is said to be converted, for positive proof that the door is not shut, thus yielding the word of God for the feelings of an individual."

---

* Sarah Harmon was five years older than her sister Ellen (Mrs. White). She married Stephen Belden, the father of F.E. Belden, the musician of Seventh-day Adventists. He has the letter now.

Notice his point: If an individual had been really converted since October, 1844, it would have proved that the door was not shut. Hence the shut door meant that there could be no genuine conversions after 1844. This was at the close of 1849, five years after 1844, published and endorsed by Mr. and Mrs. White! How does this agree with the idea that Mrs. White, all through these five years, was laboring for the conversion of sinners, as has been claimed? Why did she not refute Holt by pointing to sinners she had herself converted during this five years? Will Adventists explain?

In the same paper (pp. 41-46, same month, Dec. 16, 1849) is an article covering six pages by Elder David Arnold, entitled "The Shut Door Explained." Surely this should make the matter plain as to what was meant by the "shut door." The burden of his whole argument is that, after 1844, Christ was a mediator for saints only, and that, as the door was then shut, there had not been, nor could there be, a genuine conversion of a sinner since that time. Here are a few lines: "The professed conversions through the instrumentality of different sects are urged as positive proof that the door is not shut. I can not give up the clear fulfillment of prophecy in our experience, which shows the shut door in the past, for the opinions, fancies and feelings of men, based upon human sympathy and a superstitious reverence for early imbibed views...These professed converts will not rise to a better state than the low standard of the fallen sects; therefore, they are converted to the religion of the various sects, but not to God."

Here this writer argues exactly as does Holt, that a genuine conversion would prove the door not shut; but there had been no true conversions since 1844. That is the argument. The professed conversions were all spurious. Again we ask, Why did not Mrs. White point to her converts and refute such an argument? Why not? Because she had none. She had not labored for any. She did not believe it possible to make any. She agreed with Holt and Arnold. Remember, both articles were published in her husband's paper, edited by him.

Now let us hear Elder White upon the same question - the "shut door." In *Present Truth*, May, 1850, he has an article of

The Shut Door – Probation Ended Oct. 22, 1844

eight columns on "The Sanctuary, Twenty-three Hundred Days, and the Shut Door." In an article of such length he should be able to make his position very plain. And, indeed, he does. He uses every argument available to prove that the door of mercy was shut in 1844; and that therefore there was no intercessor and no pardon for sinners after that time. He says: "I think we shall clearly see that there can be no other place for the shut door but at the autumn of 1844...When we came up to that point of time all our sympathy, burden and prayers for sinners ceased; and the unanimous feeling and testimony was that our work for the world was finished forever...The reason that the living branches felt that their work was done, was because the twenty-three hundred days were ended, and the time had come for Jesus to shut the door of the Holy and pass into the Most Holy to receive the kingdom and cleanse the sanctuary...At this very time when the faithful servant is giving meat to the 'household' [not to the unbelieving world], and is opposed by the evil servant, and when the Advent history marked out by the parable is fulfilled, and the shut door in the past,...He is still merciful to his saints and ever will be; and Jesus is still their Advocate and Priest. But the sinner, to whom Jesus had stretched out his arms all the day long, and who had rejected the offer of salvation, was left without an advocate when Jesus passed from the Holy Place and shut the door in 1844. The professed church who rejected the truth was also rejected, smitten with blindness, and now with their flocks and herds they go to seek the Lord, as still an advocate for sinners. But, says the prophet (Hos. 5:6, 7): *'They shall not find him; he hath withdrawn himself from them.* They have dealt treacherously against the Lord, for they have begotten strange children.'"

Here it is evident that Elder White used the same argument as Holt and Arnold. Jesus is an advocate for saints, but not for sinners. The door is shut against sinners. Notice that he quotes Hos. 5:6, 7, to prove it. While they believed in the shut door, this was a text they all used over and over again. It will soon be seen that Mrs. White uses it in the same way.

Now we come to the teaching of Mrs. White herself in her "visions" and revelations on this same subject. She says that an angel came to her directly from heaven and talked with her, telling her how it all was. She writes out these "visions" for the same paper in which the articles written by Holt, Arnold, and her husband all appear. She was associated with them in the same work, talked with them, heard them preach their views, read their articles, etc.

When her husband brought home that little paper, *Present Truth*, they laid each number on the floor between them and prayed over it. In *Testimony for the Church*, Vol. I., page 88, Mrs. White says: "About the same time he began to publish a small sheet entitled *Present Truth*...Always before preparing them for the post-office, we spread them before the Lord, and prayed over them."

THE PRESENT TRUTH.

PUBLISHED SEMI-MONTHLY—BY JAMES WHITE.

Vol. 1.   MIDDLETOWN, CONN. JULY, 1849.   No. 1.

"The secret of the Lord is with them that fear him; and he will show them his covenant."—Ps. xxv. 14.

"WHEREFORE, I will not be negligent to put you always in remembrance of these things, though ye know them, and be established in the PRESENT TRUTH." 2 Pet. i: 12.

It is through the truth that souls are sanctified, and made ready to enter the everlasting kingdom. Obedience to the truth will kill us to this world, that we may be made alive, by faith in Jesus. "Sanctify them through thy truth; thy word is truth." John xvii: 17. This was the prayer of Jesus. "I have no greater joy than to hear that my children walk in truth." 3 John iv.

Error, darkness and fetters the mind, but the truth brings with it freedom, and gives light and life. True charity, or LOVE, "rejoiceth in the truth." Cor. xiii: 6. "Thy law is the truth." Ps. cxix: 142.

David describing the day of slaughter, when the pestilence shall walk in darkness, and destruction waste at noon-day, so that, "a thousand shall fall at thy side and ten thousand at thy right hand," says—

"He shall cover thee with his feathers, and under his wings shalt thou trust; his TRUTH shall be thy SHIELD and BUCKLER." Ps. xci: 4.

The storm is coming. War, famine and pestilence are already in the field of slaughter. Now is the time, the only time to seek a shelter in the truth of the living God.

In Peter's time there was present truth, or truth applicable to that present time. The Church have ever had a present truth. The present truth now, is that which shows present duty, and the right position for us who are about to witness the time of trouble, such as never was. Present truth must be oft repeated, even to those who are established in it. This was needful in the Apostles day, and it certainly is no less important for us, who are living just before the close of time.

For months I have felt burdened with the duty of writing, and publishing the present truth for the scattered flock; but the way has not been opened for me to commence the work until now. I tremble at the word of the Lord, and the importance of this time. What is done to spread the truth must be done quickly. The four Angels are holding the angry nations in check but a few days, until the saints are sealed; then the nations will rush, like the rushing of many waters. Then it will be too late to spread before precious souls, the present saving, living truths of the Holy Bible. My spirit is drawn out after the scattered remnant. May God help them to receive the truth, and be established in it. May they haste to take shelter beneath the "covering of Almighty God," is my prayer.

The Weekly Sabbath Instituted at Creation, and not at Sinai.

"And on the seventh day GOD ended his work which he had made; and he rested on the seventh day from all his work which he had made. And GOD blessed the seventh day, and sanctified it: because that in it he had rested from all his work which GOD created and made." Gen. ii: 2, 3.

Here GOD instituted the weekly rest or Sabbath. It was the seventh day. He BLESSED and SANCTIFIED that day of the week, and no other; therefore the seventh day, and no other day of the week is holy, sanctified time.

GOD has given the reason why he blessed and sanctified the seventh day. "Because that in it he had rested from all his work which GOD had created and made." He rested, and set the example for man. He blessed and set apart the seventh day for man to rest from his labor, and follow the example of his Creator. The Lord of the Sabbath said, Mark ii: 27. "The Sabbath was made for man." Not for the Jew only, but for MAN, in its broadest sense; meaning all mankind. The word man in this text, means the same as it does in the following texts. "Man that is born of a woman is of few days and full of trouble." Job xiv: 1. "Man lieth down and riseth not, till the heavens be no more." Job xiv: 12.

No one will say that man here means

The Shut Door – Probation Ended Oct. 22, 1844

She herself had articles in many of these little sheets, right along with the others. It is certain that she read each article, and knew, without doubt, what the others wrote and taught. She certainly agreed with these articles or she would not have prayed over them as she says she did.

We will quote from only one or two of her articles to show that she taught as they all did–that there was no salvation for sinners after 1844. Opening to No. 3 (August, 1849, pp. 21, 22), we discover that she claims to have been taken up to the Holy City. In relating the "vision" given her there, she says: "There I was shown that the commandments of God and the testimony of Jesus Christ, relating to the shut door, could not be separated."

She "saw" all about how in 1844 Jesus left the Holy Place and entered the Most Holy, etc. Her arguments are the same as those of all the others. She saw that the power manifested by the other churches in revivals was only the power of the devil, not the power of God. Continuing, she says: "I saw that the mysterious signs and wonders and false reformations would increase and spread. The reformations that were shown me were not reformations from error to truth, but from bad to worse; for those who professed a change of heart had only wrapped about them a religious garb, which covered up the iniquity of a wicked heart. Some *appeared* to have been really converted, so as to deceive God's people; but if their hearts could be seen, they would appear as black as ever. My accompanying angel bade me look for the travail of soul for sinners, as used to be. I looked, but could not see it, for the time for their salvation was past."

It is painful to read the dodging, quibbling, and untruthful assertions made by her defenders to evade the plain meaning of this passage. In a few years, time, with its stern facts, compelled Mrs. White and her followers to abandon the "shut door" and "no salvation for sinners" doctrine. Not one of them believes in it now. This is conclusive proof that her revelations were not from God, but were the unreliable products of autosuggestion and an abnormal state of mind.

No holy angel ever told her what she reports, for no such being would have told her what was not so, and what the passing of time has proven untrue. Her assertion gives the lie to heavenly beings. Her professed revelations were simply the product of her own mind reflecting the teaching of those around her.

Here is another of her "visions" along the same line, in the same paper, *Present Truth*, March, 1850, page 64. She says: "The excitements and false reformations of this day do not move us, for we know that the Master of the house rose up in 1844 and shut the door of the first apartment of the heavenly tabernacle; and now we certainly expect that they will go with their flocks to seek the Lord; but they shall not find him; he hath withdrawn himself (within the second veil) from them. The Lord has shown me that the power that is with them is a mere human influence, and not the power of God."

Here she quotes Hos. 5:6, 7, the same text so often used by all the others, to prove that there were no real conversions after 1844. It is idle, therefore, to say that she did not agree with the others, or to deny that she taught the shut door doctrine, the same as they. What reason does she give to explain why there were no real conversions after 1844? Note her words: Because "the Master of the house rose up in 1844 and shut the door."

In a report of labor in the *Advent Review,* May 15, 1850, Elder White, in noticing the death of a Sister Hastings, says: "She embraced the Sabbath in 1846, and has ever believed that the work of warning the world closed in 1844." This shows that they held to the shut-door idea for years after 1844.

In the *Review and Herald,* Aug. 19, 1851, Joseph Bates says: "We understand that he [Christ] was a Mediator for all the world, ministering in the Holy Place (Heb. 9:26), in the Tabernacle called the Sanctuary, from the day of Pentecost (A.D. 31) until his appointed time, the end of the twenty-three hundred days, or years–the fall of 1844. At this point of time, then, the door was shut against the Sardis church [the Protestant church] and the wicked world."

But to make still more certain that Mrs. White herself taught this repulsive, unscriptural, and fanatical doctrine, we quote further from her; this time from her "vision" at Camden, N.Y., June 29, 1851: "Then I saw that Jesus prayed for his enemies; but that should not cause *us* to pray for the wicked world, whom

THE SHUT DOOR – PROBATION ENDED OCT. 22, 1844

God has rejected. When he prayed for his enemies, there was hope for them, and they *could be benefited* and saved by his prayers, and also after he was a mediator in the outer apartment for the whole world; but *now* his spirit and sympathy were withdrawn from the world; and our sympathy must be with Jesus, and must be withdrawn from the ungodly...I saw that the wicked could not be benefited by our prayers *now*."

The genuineness of this vision is acknowledged by Editor Uriah Smith and Elder J.N. Loughborough in their efforts to explain it away. Mrs. White's defenders try to limit this message to only one person there present. But her language is too plain for such a dodging of the issue. Hear her once more on this subject. After Jesus left the Holy Place, she says: "I did not see one ray of light pass from Jesus to the careless multitude after he arose, and they were left in perfect darkness...Satan appeared to be by the throne trying to carry on the work of God. I saw them look up to the throne and pray, 'Father, give us thy spirit;' then Satan would breathe upon them an unholy influence." (*Early Writings,* pp. 55, 56; ed. 1907.)

Her teaching here is as clear as day–not one ray of light comes to sinners since 1844, but all are left to the devil! What is the use of Adventists denying that she taught this doctrine? She certainly did teach it.

THEIR DENIAL OF THESE PLAIN FACTS

Now notice how Adventists squarely deny all this. Elder Butler, in *Replies to Canright,* page 100, says that neither Mrs. White nor any of them ever taught that there was no salvation for sinners after 1844. Then he adds: "It is a slander to say the contrary. We also declare, with no fear of contradiction, that during this very period, when Elder C. and other opposers of the same ilk taught that she and others believed that there was no salvation for sinners, she and they were laboring for the conversion of sinners."

We here and now flatly deny every word of Elder Butler's statement, and confidently refer all to the quotations already given from Holt, Arnold, Bates, White, and Mrs. White herself, in refutation of what he asserts. The statements are plain. The reader can judge for himself who is telling the truth.

Moreover, we deny that Mrs. White, or any of their ministers during these years named, ever made the slightest effort to convert even one sinner. To have done so would have contradicted all their arguments. Let them produce one line in evidence of one case where Mrs. White, or any of them, labored to convert a common sinner. No reference to such a case can be found in any of their published works of that date. On the contrary, the publications of that early time are full of unquestionable evidence that they did not labor to convert any one, for the very reason that they believed it futile.

Elder White, her husband, taught the same things she did at this period in their history. In *Present Truth*, page 69, dated April, 1850, he said: "Babylon, the nominal church is fallen. God's people have come out of her. She is now the 'synagogue of Satan.' (Rev. 3:9.) 'The habitation of devils, and the hold of every foul spirit, and the cage of every unclean and hateful bird.' (Rev. 18:2.)"

Yes, after 1844 all the Protestant churches were wholly left of God, turned over to Satan, who answered their prayers! They were all only the abode of devils and corruption! Yet these very churches, since that time, have produced a Spurgeon, a Livingstone, a Bishop Simpson, a Moody, and at least one-third of all the devout members of the Seventh-day Adventist Church itself! A large share of their own members were first converted in the "synagogue of Satan," and Adventists very gladly received them into their church as good Christians!

Even the devil seems to be pushing the propaganda of conversion for them, through the churches that are "the habitation of devils, and the hold of every foul spirit, and the cage of every unclean and hateful bird."

How utterly inconsistent is the association of the young missionary students of the Seventh-day Adventist people with the student volunteers of the other Christian bodies, if they believe and remain loyal to the "visions" of Mrs. White and the teachings of her husband and other early Advent leaders. They are still privately calling upon the converts of the "devil-filled"

The Shut Door – Probation Ended Oct. 22, 1844

churches to "come out" of them, and publicly professing to show a spirit of fellowship toward these churches, while in reality remaining hostile to them.

These earnest Adventist young people are unaware of these early positions of their church, supported by the revelations of the woman whom they are taught to place by the side of the greatest prophets and apostles of past ages. They only need to investigate with open mind, to reject the whole scheme, and come to the simple basis of loyalty to Christ and his apostles, as the real leaders and teachers of the church.

Did Christ and the Holy Spirit lead these founders of the Seventh-day Adventist Church to lose for years all their burden and sympathy for sinners and cease to pray for them?

Was Christ in sympathy with them when they taught that he no longer was a friend of sinners?

Was he in sympathy with them when they taught that he was no longer an advocate for them, and that the whole world was rejected of God, left without the Holy Spirit, turned over to Satan, and that all churches save their own were only the synagogue of Satan, forts of the devil, in fact?

Did a holy angel tell Mrs. White all that terribly false message?

Such a theory seems like blasphemy. If God did not lead them then, has he led them since? Is he leading them now?

How the Shut Door Was Opened

In *Present Truth* for April, 1850, page 72, is an account of an effort to save "the children of the remnant." This was six years after the "door was shut" in 1844. In these six years some of their own children had grown to years of accountability, unsaved.

Here was a new experience, an unlooked-for difficulty. How could they get these, their own children, in through that "shut door"?

"Necessity is the mother of invention." Here is the way they fixed it up for their children: "As they [little children] were then [1844] in a state of *innocence*, they were entitled to a record upon the breastplate of judgment as much as those who had sinned and received pardon; and are, therefore subjects of the present intercession of our great high priest" (*Present Truth*, p. 45.)

This, of course, was pure assumption, without a particle of Scriptural proof; but it "did the business"! The children of "the remnant"–that is, their children–went in to Holy of Holies on the breastplate of Jesus in 1844! They were inside, and, therefore, could repent and be saved later!

This was the first slight modification of the "shut door" doctrine held by the Seventh-day Adventists. Soon another unexpected event occurred which compelled them to open the door a little wider. In *Replies to Canright*, page 102, Elder Butler gives an account of it.

In 1850 a Mr. Churchill was accepted as a converted man. Butler says: "His was one of the very first cases of conversion from the world to the present truth which occurred after 1844. As we have said, their work hitherto had been almost wholly for the 'lost sheep of the house of Israel'–the old Advent believers...He [Churchill] had married after this [1844] a daughter of Sister Benson, a '44 Adventist...They were quite surprised at first that one who had been an unbeliever should manifest an interest in the Advent doctrine...His conversion was noised abroad quite extensively."

Study this carefully. Butler says that their work had been almost wholly for "old Advent believers." It had not been almost, but entirely, for old Adventists. They had not paid the slightest attention to any outside body of old believers. Mr. Churchill's conversion "surprised" them, and it was "noised abroad extensively." His was the very first conversion from the world after 1844; that is, six years after.

This is a confession that for six years after 1844 they had not converted a single sinner. Had Mrs. White and all the able ministers been laboring for years for sinners without making a single convert? She claims over and over that the power of the Holy Spirit was upon her all that time. Was this the proof of it?

Again, why were they surprised at this first conversion? Why was it so extensively commented on? The reason is plain. It was unexpected and contrary to their previous views. Fur-

The Shut Door – Probation Ended Oct. 22, 1844

ther, did they seek Churchill and labor for him? No! He came seeking admittance without being invited. As he was son-in-law to the church, as in the case of their own children, the door was opened a little more, and he was let in!

Then again, it was drawing near to the time (1851) when they were compelled to abandon the "shut door" theory. Evidently this Churchill conversion, and the case of their own children growing up, began to open their eyes to the folly of their "shut door" views, and caused them to hasten their modification and finally give them up entirely.

The following extract is taken from the *Review and Herald* under date of June 11, 1861, and signed by nine of their prominent ministers: "Our views of the work before us were then mostly vague and indefinite, some still retaining the idea adopted by the body of Advent believers in 1844, with Wm. Miller at their head, that our work for the world was finished, and that the message was confined to those of the original Advent faith. So firmly was this believed that one of our number was nearly refused the message, the individual presenting it having doubts of the possibility of his salvation, because he was not in the '44 movement."

Until well along in 1851, their whole effort was in the interest of the old Advent believers only. All of their writings during that period are full of this teaching. In *Present Truth*, May, 1850, Elder White says: "This work of bringing out the jewels and purifying away error is fast increasing, and is destined to move on with increasing power until the saints are all searched out and receive the seal of the living God."

You see, they conceived their work to be that of searching out "the jewels," "the saints," not sinners. Their first publication of 1847 was *To the Little Flock*. Then all through everything they published from that time on until well into the year 1851, their articles are addressed to "believers," "the little flock," "the remnant," "the scattered flock," "the torn flock," "to the household of faith," "to scattered jewels," "to the saints," "to the honest in heart," etc.

On page 72 of *Present Truth*, Mrs. White says: "The swift messengers must speed on their way to search out the scattered flock." Nowhere in all those years do we find one word about going to seek sinners or to labor for them. Hence their surprise when a sinner came to them of his own accord and sought admission. It was a wonder heralded widespread to all the church.

The truth is that their early publications contain so much of their "shut door" teaching that is has been difficult to decide what to publish and what to omit. Much has necessarily been omitted to economize space.

Here is one more item of evidence that their work for years after 1844 was confined to seeking out only those who had been in the 1844 movement. It is taken from the *Review and Herald*, Sept. 7, 1916: "For nearly ten years the work was confined to the gathering in of those who had accepted the first angel's message." (Miller's work.)

Exactly. Their work in those first years after '44 was not to seek sinners, but old Advent Christians, as this article confesses.

SEVENTH-DAY ADVENTISTS HOLD KEY TO DOOR OF MERCY

Fanaticism dies hard. After 1851 they began to open that "shut door" so that now all could get in conditionally. They must understand the sanctuary in heaven, the change Jesus made in 1844 from the Holy to the Most Holy, and follow him in there by faith. Praying to him anywhere else was only to be lost! So says Mrs. White in *Early Writings*, edition 1907, page 261: "They have no other knowledge of the move made in heaven, or the way into the Most Holy, and they can not be benefited by the intercession of Jesus there...They offer up their useless prayers to the apartment which Jesus has left."

Defending this view, Elder Uriah Smith, in *Objections to the Visions Answered*, published in 1868, pages 24-26, says: " A knowledge of Christ's position and work is necessary to the enjoyment of the benefits of his mediation...A general idea of his work was then [previous to 1844] sufficient to enable men to approach unto God by him...But when he changed his position [in 1844] to the Most Holy Place...that knowledge of his work which had up to that point been sufficient, was no longer sufficient...Who can find salvation now? Those who go to the Sav-

The Shut Door – Probation Ended Oct. 22, 1844

iour where he is and view him by faith in the Most Holy Place...This is the door now open for salvation. But no man can understand this change without definite knowledge of the subject of the sanctuary and the relation of type and antitype. Now they may seek the Saviour as they have before sought him, with no other idea of his position and ministry than those which they entertained while he was in the first apartment; but will it avail them? They will not find him there. That door is shut."

This theory is about as bad as the original "shut door." To find salvation now a sinner must understand the change Jesus made up in heaven in 1844. But who knows about this? Only Seventh-day Adventists. The whole world and all Christendom are totally ignorant of that change. Therefore, all these were hopelessly lost, for their prayers never reached where Jesus was!

It is almost beyond human comprehension that sane people would teach such views; but here you have them over their own signatures. In Mrs. White's *Early Writings* they still give out to their people these statements as the inspired word of God!

The author has conversed with individuals who positively affirm that they have heard Mrs. White repeatedly teach this shut door doctrine. There are even some still living who will under oath declare that they have heard her advocate it.

Signed Testimony

John Megquier, Sago, Maine, a man noted for his integrity, writes: "We well know the course of Ellen G. White, the visionist, while in the state of Maine. About the first visions she had were at my house in Poland. She said that God had told her in vision that the door of mercy had closed, and there was no more chance for the world." (*The True Sabbath,* by Miles Grant, p. 70.)

Mrs. L.S. Burdick, San Francisco, Cal., was well acquainted with Mrs. White. She writes: "I became acquainted with James White and Ellen Harmon (now Mrs. White) early in 1845...Ellen was having what was called visions: said that God had shown her in vision that Jesus Christ arose and on the tenth day of the seventh month, 1844, shut the door of mercy; had left forever the mediatorial throne; the whole world was doomed and lost; and there never could be another sinner saved." (*The True Sabbath*, p. 72.)

These persons knew the facts, and have put their testimony on record. It has been made apparent to every unprejudiced reader that both Mrs. White and her husband, James White, clearly taught that the Holy Spirit was withdrawn from the world and the "nominal" churches in 1844. All of them were left "without reprovings of conscience." Satan answered their prayers. Their prayers to God were useless.

That was over seventy years ago–two generations. Since that date (1844) scores, hundreds, thousands, of the most devoted, consecrated men and women the world had ever known, have grown up, been converted, and devoted their lives and their all to the work of saving souls. Thousands of these have gone into the darkest regions of heathenism and have worn themselves out for Christ and his church. Many of these have been imprisoned, beaten, or slain for the sake of Christ and his gospel. They have endured as great sufferings and accomplished as great a work as the apostles themselves did.

Besides these who have given all, are thousands who have willingly contributed millions of wealth to help the missionaries forward the work of bringing the heathen from darkness to light. One case like that of David Livingstone in Africa, or of Charles Spurgeon in England, or of D.L. Moody in America, gives lie to the above teachings of Mrs. White and her colaborers.

The work of Adventists themselves in laboring for the salvation of sinners now contradicts her statement that the Spirit of God left the world in 1844. An editorial in their own paper, the *Advent Review*, Sept. 23, 1915, has this truthful statement: "As never before, perhaps, in the history of the world, did there exist such a spirit of reaching after God." This squarely contradicts Mrs. White's assertion that the Spirit of God was withdrawn from the world in 1844.

The Shut Door – Probation Ended Oct. 22, 1844

The Results of Fanaticism

In the study of this chapter we see some of the evils that result from fanaticism; how one error paves the way for another; and how loath men are to give up fanatical views. The error of time-setting in 1844 led to the misapplication of the parable of the ten virgins; the misapplication of the parable led to the theory of the "shut door," or no mercy for sinners after 1844; and this led to a misunderstanding of the sanctuary in heaven, the atonement, and Christ's mediatorial work, and the whole movement led to the unchristianizing of the whole Christian world.

But time has compelled them to change their views, if not their bigotry and exclusiveness. From holding that God no longer had a merciful message of salvation for the world, Adventists have come to believe that they are the only people that have a message for the world today.

From the belief that the door of mercy was closed to the world in 1844, they have passed to the belief that they are the only people who hold the key that will unlock this door.

From holding erroneous views regarding the subject of the sanctuary, many of which with the lapse of time they have been forced to abandon, they have come to hold that they are the only people who understand the sanctuary question.

Because the Protestant churches did not accept the time-setting views of William Miller, Seventh-day Adventists have held and still hold that these churches are the "Babylon" of Rev. 14:8, which is fallen. Believing thus, it has been impossible for them to associate with the members of these churches as fellow Christians.

From first to last, their views have led them to shut some door in the face of everybody, even the most earnest Christian workers in the world. Mrs. White's professed revelations from God place, for them, the stamp of divine approval upon all such attitudes upon their part, and her fanatical theories, all proclaimed as revelations from God, have made the fanaticism of these people most difficult to uproot.

WILLIAM MILLER

𝔇amaging 𝔚ritings 𝔖uppressed

We have shown in the chapter on the "shut door" that Mrs. White, with all other early Seventh-day Adventists, strongly taught that, from Oct. 22, 1844, until the same time in 1851, there was no salvation for sinners.

A few months before this seven years ended, Elder White and his wife became convinced that this theory had to be given up. Therefore, at Saratoga Springs, N.Y., in August, 1851, Elder White, with his wife, published *Experience and Views*, a little pamphlet of sixty-four pages. No reference by either of them is made in this to *A Word to the Little Flock*, published by James White in 1847, nor to *Present Truth*, published in 1849 and 1850, although all but seven introductory pages of *Experience and Views* is copied word for word from these two publications.

Why this studied silence regarding these two publications? Because both of these old works were full of the "shut door" theory. Hence it was necessary to have these quietly dropped out of sight and forgotten as soon as possible. This is the explanation of their having been kept out of sight ever since.

They will never be seen by the younger generation of Seventh-day Adventists with the consent of the leaders who now know that they once existed. A knowledge of them would absolutely destroy the faith of intelligent and honest believers in Mrs. White, in any of her claims, and this would mean the destruction of the very heart and soul of the denominational life.

In 1882 the office at Battle Creek, Mich., published a small work entitled *Early Writings* by Mrs. White. In the preface the publishers say: "A widespread interest has arisen in all her works, especially in these early views, and the call for the publication of a second edition has become imperative." "No portion of the work has been omitted. No shadow of change has been made in any idea or sentiment of the original work; and the verbal changes have been made under the author's own eye and with her full approval."

In the *Advent Review* of Dec. 26, 1882, is an article from the pen of Elder G.I. Butler, under the caption, "A Book Long Desired." In this article he calls the attention of his readers to the importance of purchasing the foregoing-mentioned book. From this article we make the following quotations: "These were the very first of the published writings of Sister White...Many have greatly desired to have in their possession ALL she has written for publication...So strong was the interest to have these early writings reproduced that several years ago the General Conference recommended by vote that they be republished. The volume under consideration is the result of this interest. It meets a long felt want...There is another interesting feature connected with this matter. The enemies of this cause, who have spared no pains to break down the faith of our people in the testimonies of God's Spirit and the interest felt in the writings of Sister White, have made all the capital possible from the fact that her early writings were not attainable. They have said many things about our 'suppressing' these writings, as if we were ashamed of them. Some have striven to make it appear that there was something objectionable about them, that we feared would come to the light of day, and that we carefully kept them in the background. These lying insinuations have answered their purpose in deceiving some unwary souls. They now appear in their real character, by the publication of several thousand copies of this 'suppressed' book, which our enemies pretended we were very anxious to conceal. They have claimed to be very anxious to obtain these writings to show their supposed error. They now have the opportunity."

Immediately after *Early Writings* was published, Elder A.C. Long published a tract of sixteen pages entitled *Comparison of the Early Writings of Mrs. White with Later Publications*. We here present a quotation from Mr. Long's tract: "From the above quotations we gather the following points: First, these 'Early Writings' of Mrs. White were published under her eye and with her full approval. Second, they contain ALL her early visions. Third, those who have claimed that certain portions of her early visions were 'suppressed' are liars, since they are now all re-republished."

We now present the evidence to show that the foregoing quotation, in which Elder Butler says that the work he speaks of contains ALL of Mrs. White's "early writings" is absolutely untrue and deceptive. The earliest writings of Mrs. White were published by Elder White in 1847, in a small pamphlet of only twenty-four pages, entitled *A Word to the Little Flock*. The work to which Elder Butler refers, as containing all of her early writings, published in 1882, claims to be an exact reprint of all her early visions.

Now note carefully that, commencing at the beginning of her first vision, as published in 1847, we read down thirty-three lines and discover that the late republished work agrees with the old on nearly word for word, only a few slight changes without altering the sense. But at the end of the thirty-third line we find that four lines have been omitted or "suppressed." These read as follows: "It was just as impossible for them [those who gave up their faith in the 1844 movement] to get on the path again and go to the city, AS ALL THE WICKED WORLD WHICH GOD HAD REJECTED. They fell all along the

G.I. BUTLER

path, one after another."

These lines are found on page 14 of the edition of 1847. They are not to be found in the later editions of the visions published in 1851 and in 1882. We have all three editions in our possession. Why were these few lines left out? Because at the 1847 date Mrs. White believed in the "shut door" theory, and claimed that by divine revelation God had shown her that "*all the wicked world which God had rejected*" was lost forever. In the autumn of 1851 and in 1882 she no longer believed that theory; hence these lines had to be omitted.

Here God's professed prophetic messenger dared to tamper with an alleged divine revelation.

Now, reading on seventy-two lines farther in this vision, we discover twenty-two more lines to have been omitted. Here are a few of them: "In a moment we were winging our way upwards; and, entering in, here we saw good old father Abraham, Isaac, Jacob, Noah, Daniel, and many like them."

At that early date Mrs. White still believed in the conscious state of the dead; so she sees all these patriarchs in heaven. Later she discarded that idea for the theory that the dead are unconscious in the sleep of death. It therefore becomes plain why these lines were omitted. She had changed her views on the state of the dead, and therefore this "revelation" of God to her must go.

A little further on two lines are omitted; still farther on eight lines are left out; and nine lines yet farther on in the vision. A vision which Mrs. White had at Camden, N.Y., June 29, 1851, is entirely missing from this volume which professes to include ALL of Mrs. White's early writings.

Here is a quotation from this suppressed vision: "Then I saw that Jesus prayed for his enemies; but that should not cause US or lead US to pray for THE WICKED WORLD, WHOM GOD HAD REJECTED. When he prayed for his enemies, there was hope for them, and they COULD BE BENEFITED AND SAVED BY HIS PRAYERS, and also after he was a mediator, in the outer apartment for the whole world; BUT NOW HIS SPIRIT AND SYMPATHY WERE WITHDRAWN FROM THE WORLD; AND OUR SYMPATHY MUST BE WITH JESUS, AND MUST BE

Damaging Writings Suppressed

WITHDRAWN FROM THE UNGODLY."

The reason why this vision was suppressed is plain. It taught the shut-door doctrine in the plainest terms. Why, then, should Elder Butler accuse those who had called the attention of a deluded people to the fact that some of Mrs. White's writings and visions had been suppressed, of making "lying insinuations" against her and her colaborers?

Here are the facts. They have never been, nor can they be, successfully refuted. It is clearly manifest why all these "inspired" statements and visions were suppressed. They taught the shut-door doctrine, and said that the Adventist people were not to "*pray for the wicked world which God had rejected*"; that their sympathy "*must be withdrawn from the ungodly.*" After 1844 they were to have no sympathy for the ungodly, nor must the pray for them!

The most important work published by the Seventh-day Adventists during the years in which they believed and taught that probation had closed for sinners in 1844, was a paper called *Present Truth*. There were eleven numbers of this printed. They were issued from various places in the East, covering the period from July, 1849, to November, 1850.

In the number for August, 1849, pages 21 to 24, is a long vision by Mrs. White. This vision is reproduced in *Early Writings*, edition 1882, pages 34 to 37, except eight lines from page 22, relating to reformations since 1844, which are omitted. These lines are as follows: "But from bad to worse; for those who professed a change of heart had only wrapped about them a religious garb which covered up the iniquity of a wicked heart. Some appeared to have been fully converted, so as to deceive God's people; but if their hearts could be seen, they would appear as black as ever."

The reason why these lines were suppressed is plain. They teach in the strongest language possible that there were no real conversions after 1844. In 1882 they no longer believed this; so these lines had to be suppressed.

On pages 31 and 32 of *Present Truth* is another long vision by Mrs. White. This vision is quoted on pages 37 to 39 of *Early Writings*. Here, again, thirty-five lines are suppressed. The omis-

omission is so lengthy we quote only a part of it simply to show why the omission was made. In this, she says the messengers sent out of God *"would be safe from the prevailing pestilence. But if any went that were not sent of God, they would be in danger of being cut down by the pestilence...What we have seen and heard of the pestilence is but the beginning of what we shall see and hear. Soon the dead and dying will be all around us."*

The pestilence here referred to was local, brief, and soon checked. No such thing happened as she predicted. She simply expressed the fears common to frighten persons at the time. That is all. The vision absolutely failed, and therefore these lines had to be suppressed!

Continuing on to page 64 of *Present Truth*, we there find another vision which has been entirely omitted from her *Early Writings*. The motive for the omission will be apparent to all. A portion of the vision runs as follows: "The excitements and false reformations of this day do not move us, for we know that the Master of the house rose up in 1844, and shut the door of the first apartment of the heavenly tabernacle; and now we certainly expect that they will go with their flocks to seek the Lord; but they shall not find him; he hath withdrawn himself (within the second veil) from them. The Lord has shown me that the power that is with them is a mere human influence and not the power of God."

Mrs. White here quotes Hos. 5:6,7 to prove that there were no genuine conversions after 1844. This, all their ministers did at this time, as has been seen already. She "saw" just what all the others saw.

Again, in *Present Truth*, November, 1850, pages 86 and 87, there are nearly three columns in fine print, recording another of Mrs. White's visions. Almost two whole columns of this vision are omitted from *Early Writings*. (See pp. 63-65.) All of the omitted passages here quoted or referred to are in the very first writings of Mrs. White.

Early Writings, published in 1882, claims to contain all the early writings of Mrs. White, with *"NOT A WORD OMITTED."* If this claim were true, all of the omitted passages here quoted and referred to would be included. But they are not.

DAMAGING WRITINGS SUPPRESSED

Why were they suppressed? The answer has already been given.

What, then, shall we say of the publishers' statement? Is it not a deliberate misrepresentation of fact, made to hide some of Mrs. White's "inspired" erroneous teachings?

In *Early Writings,* edition of 1882, we read: "Preface to the FIRST edition. James White, August, 1851." Was the first edition that of 1851? No, indeed! The FIRST edition of her early writings was issued in 1847. Then, again, in this 1882 edition, we read: "This SECOND edition," etc. This statement is also untrue, because that was the THIRD edition of her early writings.

This was done by Elder and Mrs. White, to keep out of sight the dangerous first edition of 1847. As this was all done with Mrs. White's approval, and as it was copyrighted by her, did she not know that these statements were not true? Surely she did.

But Elder Butler was not aware of it. Up to 1882, the edition of 1851 was the only one of which he knew, and so, of course, he copied from that edition, word for word, just as he said. As soon, however, as the edition of 1882 was published, Elder A.C. Long issued his pamphlet, giving all the passages omitted from the edition of 1847. Butler read this. Mrs. White also knew of it. Honesty in either, or both of them, required that an apology be made, and that the omitted passages immediately be printed as addenda to be sent with the remaining copies, or at least be printed in the next edition.

But what has occurred? Thirty-five years have gone by, eleven editions have been printed, thousands of copies are still being sold to the uninformed people, and yet no reference has been made to these known suppressed passages, nor has a line of any of them been inserted in later editions. Every copy sent out states what the publishers now know to be false. All this justifies our charge that there is a streak of deception in the whole work of Seventh-day Adventists, from first to last.

The *Review and Herald,* Aug. 17, 1916, says, "No religious body has ever come upon the stage of action but needed to carefully consider its rise and progress."

The two very earliest publications of Seventh-day Adventists–namely, *A Word to the Little Flock*, 1847, and *Present Truth*, 1849-1850–are withheld by their leaders from their people. Why are they withheld? To suppress the false teachings of Mrs. White contained in them, which prove her writings uninspired. That is why.

In the providence of God, the author happens to know the inside facts regarding the publication of *Early Writings* in 1882. For years he had been closely connected with Elder White and his wife, Elders Butler, Smith, and others. At that time Butler was president of the General Conference, president of the Publishing Association, etc.

One day in 1880 he came into the office where Elder Smith and myself were. In high glee he said: "Those Western rebels say we have suppressed some of Sister White's earliest visions. I will stop their mouths, for I am going to republish all she ever wrote in those early visions."

Elder White leaned forward, dropped his voice low, and said, "Butler, you better go a little slow." That was all. I did not understand what his warning meant, nor did Butler.

Soon Elder White died–in August, 1881. Butler then went ahead, and in 1882 issued the present edition of *Early Writings*. In the preface he said not a word of her early writings had been omitted. The book, he said, contained all she had written. Then, as already stated, came Elder Long's exposure of that untrue statement, in which he gave numerous passages from *A Word to the Little Flock*, which had been suppressed. This put Butler in a bad light.

At that time Elder U. Smith and myself were on the most intimate terms. We both agreed in having little confidence in Mrs. White's inspiration. So it pleased Smith to have Butler pricked on that point, and have the visions put in doubt.

Under date of March 22, 1883, Elder Smith, formerly a staunch defender of Mrs. White, wrote me thus: "I was interested in your queries to Uncle George [Butler] on the omissions in *Early Writings*. We have the Marion paper in exchange, and I noticed the article. Under the circumstances, I think it must have come down on him like an avalanche...I have no doubt the quotations are correct. I remember coming across the tract, *A Word to the Little Flock*, when we were in Rochester, but I have not seen a copy since, and did not know but *Experience and Views* [1851] contained the full text of the early visions...After the unjust treatment I have received [from Mrs. White] the past year, I feel no burden in that direction [that is, to defend the visions]."

Notice: Smith began work in the *Review* office at Rochester, N.Y., in 1855. There he saw a copy of *A Word to the Little Flock*. In 1883 he had not seen one since; that is, in twenty-eight years. And this in face of the fact that he was in the *Review* office, their leading publishing-house, as editor-in-chief, all those years.

The second edition of Mrs. White's *Early Writings* was published by Elder and Mrs. White in 1851. Smith supposed, as all others did, that this contained all she had written in 1847. But it did not. If Elder Smith had not seen that book in twenty-eight years, what opportunity had Butler and others to see it?

I was closely associated with that work for twenty-five years. I collected every book, pamphlet and tract they had ever published that could be found. I had the unbound works bound into volumes, and now have five of these, including the very earliest publications I could find. But I never saw a copy of *A Word to the Little Flock* or *Present Truth*, their very first publications, until later–did not know that either existed.

As shown in the chapter on "The Shut Door," Elder Bates led Elder White and his wife to believe that Jesus would end his work in the sanctuary above in seven years from Oct. 22, 1844. This period would end in 1851. Near the close of that period, it appears that Elder White and his wife saw that this theory must be abandoned. But what of their two early publications, both full of the doctrine? A study of the situation shows that they must have agreed to leave out of her writings all passages that strongly upheld that view, publish the rest of her writings under a new name, and drop their first two publications, *A Word to the Little Flock*, and *Present Truth*, out of sight as soon as they could.

A new paper was started with a new name, *Advent Review and Sabbath Herald*. In August, 1851, two months before the end of the seven years, Mrs. White herself revised what she had before written in *A Word to the Little Flock* in 1847, and in *Present Truth* in 1849-50, and left out the objectionable passages and visions already mentioned.

Here are her own words about the affair: "*Here I will give the view that was first published in 1846. In this view I saw only a very few of the events of the future. More recent views have been more full. I shall, therefore, LEAVE OUT A PORTION and prevent repetition*" (*Experience and Views*, August, 1851, p. 9.)

This reveals who did the "leaving out." It was Mrs. White herself. Then Elder White attended to the printing, as shown in the preface. Both of them, therefore, knew about and agreed to the suppressions. Any reference to the edition of 1847, or *Present Truth,* published in 1849 and 1850, is studiously avoided.

How effectually those first two publications were dropped out of sight is proven by the fact that Elder Smith had not seen the first one in twenty-eight years, and had no copy of the second as late as 1868.

In that year (1868) Elder Smith wrote a book of 144 pages in which he attempted to defend Mrs. White's visions. It is entitled *The Visions of Mrs. E.G. White.* Referring to these old publications, he says: "Is there any law compelling us to keep on hand an edition of every vision that has ever been published? We certainly wish that we had them, and could put them on sale at this office" (p. 123.) This shows that at that date they were not in the office, nor did the editor know where to get them.

He says that they would gladly put them on sale if they had them. Well, for fifty years past they have had that opportunity, but have refused to publish and sell them. Elder Smith here also confesses that they had not republished all of Mrs. White's visions, as the law did not compel them to do it!! Here Smith and Butler flatly contradict each other.

Again, on page 125, referring to the suppressed passages, he says: "As we have not proof to the contrary, we will take it for granted, as the objector claims, that these statements were published in *Present Truth,* August, 1849." Here, again, he confesses that the *Review* office had no copy of that important first volume of their first paper ever published.

This is significant. How carefully editors keep on file every number of their papers. Why was that most valuable first volume allowed to become so completely lost? Yes, why? Those old documents of 1847 to 1850 ought to be invaluable to Seventh-day Adventists, because they contain a history of the earliest days of the church, the first writings of Mrs. White and all their pioneers. How eagerly their people would buy and read them if they had the opportunity! But their eyes will never behold them if it depends upon their leaders to supply them.

Recently Elder Butler reported that at one meeting he sold about fifty full sets, of nine volumes each, of Mrs. White's *Testimonies.* They sell at about two dollars per volume, best binding—eighteen dollars per set to each family. This shows how readily her writings are purchased by her followers.

Why are they not given an opportunity to purchase and read her very first writings just as they were written and published? The reason has already been stated. The leaders know that to reproduce them would place in the hands of their people matter which would at once discredit Mrs. White's claims to inspiration. They would discover that not only had she taught error, but that she claimed divine inspiration for it. But so effectually have all these writings been suppressed, that only a few of their leading men even know of their existence. The body of their people are in absolute ignorance of them.

On Aug. 12, 1915, the author wrote to Elder F.M. Wilcox, editor of the *Review and Herald,* their leading denominational paper, urging him to republish these old works, offering to loan him copies for the purpose. Here is his answer:

> Washington, D.C.
> Aug. 17, 1915
>
> Mr. D.M. Canright
> Grand Rapids, Mich.
>
> Dear Brother:
>
> I desire to acknowledge receipt of your letter of August 12. Most of our brethren are away attending camp-meeting. It will be two or three weeks before they will be in. As soon as we can have a meeting of our board, I will call up your letter and will write you further about the matter.
>
> Yours sincerely,
> (signed) Francis M. Wilcox.

I have never heard from him since. Evidently the board decided that the wise course was to permit these old documents to rest in silence.

I knew very well that they would dare do nothing else. After waiting several months, I wrote to Elder Wilcox again, but have never received a reply. Evidently the officials decided to consign these early publications to "outer darkness," so far as Seventh-day Adventists are concerned.

Their refusal to bring these early writings to the light is the best evidence that they fear them. The chapter on "The Shut Door," in this work, explains why.

A Deliberate Deception

Elder J.N. Loughborough, in his book, *The Great Second Advent Movement,* page 263, edition 1905, desired to give Elder Joseph Bates' testimony concerning Mrs. White's work, as given on page 21 of *A Word to the Little Flock,* printed in 1847. The following illustrates the manner in which he uses the material from this early publication.

He quotes: "I believe the work [of Mrs. White] is of God, and is given to comfort and strengthen his scattered, torn and peeled people, since the closing up of our work...in October, 1844."

Note those three little dots? They mean that something was left out of the passage quoted. What was it? Just THREE SHORT WORDS. We will insert those words omitted from the lines quoted and indicate them [in uppercase letters]. Here they are: *"since the closing up of our work FOR THE WORLD in October, 1844."*

These three words reveal the fact that Bates and Elder White, who published the tract in 1847, believed that their work for the world closed up in October, 1844. Elder Loughborough wished to use these lines and yet hide this fact regarding the belief of these early leaders. To accomplish it he omitted - suppressed - just three words, and placed three dots in their place in his quotation!

He did not do this to save space in a large work of six hundred pages. He did it to hide, conceal, and suppress a doctrine

Damaging Writings Suppressed

which he well knew Bates and Elder and Mrs. White all believed and taught in 1847.

It is a deliberate deception, too plain to be denied. It shows how willing he was to falsify in order to shield Mrs. White and the pioneers in this movement who adhered to her and proclaimed her a prophet.

Here is another case in which the same writer, Elder Loughborough, deliberately suppressed several lines from Mrs. White's first vision, published in 1847. Again, he did it to shield her, and to hide the fact that she then taught that probation for the world ended in 1844. We will give this quotation, found on page 204 in his work, and enclose [in uppercase letters] the lines he left out.

Concerning those Adventists who became backsliders after 1844, Loughborough quotes Mrs. White as writing thus: They *"fell off the path down into the dark and wicked world below. IT WAS JUST AS IMPOSSIBLE FOR THEM TO GET ON THE PATH AGAIN AND GO TO THE CITY AS ALL THE WICKED WORLD WHICH GOD HAD REJECTED. Soon we heard the voice of God like many waters,"* etc.

Was it honest to suppress these lines? Most certainly not. Following in the footsteps of Elder Loughborough, Elder G.I. Butler, writing in the *Review and Herald*, Aug. 17, 1916, suppressed the same passage. He gave the same quotation, suppressed the same lines, and for the same purpose.

Butler knew that he was deceiving, for only a few years previously he had this very matter laid before him. He well knew the entire passage as it appeared in Mrs. White's early vision. In view of all the exposures that had been made of these suppressions, how could he plead ignorance?

How much reliance can be placed upon the statements of Mrs. White and these men when they undertake to defend the past history of Seventh-day Adventism? Absolutely none at all.

We are personally well acquainted with both of these men just mentioned. In ordinary business matters we would consider them perfectly truthful and absolutely reliable. We would trust either of them with any amount of money simply on their word of honor. But they furnish a sad example of a not uncommon experience; namely, that sometimes men, reliable in everything else, will quibble, dodge, and often squarely deny the plainest facts of their history in order to save a cause that has become dear to them.

Mrs. White's numerous deceptions come under the same head. Do Baptists, Methodists, Disciples, or any other evangelical church have to practice such methods to cover up past mistakes? Not one of them. All are proud of their past. But Seventh-day Adventists are ashamed of theirs, and well they may be.

In attempting to defend Mrs. White's visions as divine revelations, and in permitting her and her writings to occupy so prominent a place in their work, they have simply invited difficulties from which it is impossible for them to extricate themselves without exposing her mistakes and the falsity of her claims. In order to cover up her mistakes, they stultify themselves and harden their own consciences. They become practical Jesuits.

STILL AT IT

In the General Conference vault in the office at their headquarters at Washington, D.C., are many thousands of pages of Mrs. White's unpublished writing. These are carefully guarded from their own people. It is claimed, however, that every line of these writings was inspired by the Holy Ghost to guide that people now. Yet they are withheld from them by the officials. Why do they do this? What right have they to withhold all these writings if they are God's inspired words?

Recently some of their workers in their printing-office were given access to this vault. They discovered these hidden writings, and copied hundreds of pages of them. When the officials learned of this, they demanded that the copies that had been made be given up, with the threat that these brethren would lose their jobs if they refused.

Three of them yielded; but two–Claude E. Holmes and Frank Hayes–refused to do so. Holmes, an expert linotypist, was promptly dismissed from the office, and Hayes, an electrical engineer, is threatened with the same thing if he does not yield. This illustrates how the officials still manipulate and suppress Mrs. White's "inspired" writings to suit their purpose. And still they make faith in the inspiration of these writings a test of fellowship in the church!

Lastly, what prophet of God ever suppressed his own inspired writings? This one test alone is sufficient to disprove Mrs. White's claims to divine inspiration.

𝔓𝔥𝔦𝔩𝔬𝔰𝔬𝔭𝔥𝔶 𝔬𝔣 𝔥𝔢𝔯 𝔙𝔦𝔰𝔦𝔬𝔫𝔰

The proof is abundant that Mrs. White's visions were merely the result of her early misfortune, nervous disease, and a complication of hysteria, epilepsy, catalepsy, and ecstasy. That she may have honestly believed in them herself does not alter the fact.

The writer personally knew four other women, all Seventh-day Adventists, who likewise had visions. All were sincere Christians and fully believed in their own visions. But all were sickly, nervous, and hysterical. Not being encouraged in them, but opposed by their ministers, they finally gave them up.

In every age such cases have been numerous. A few of them, like Mrs. Southcott, Mrs. Ann Lee, and Mrs. White, have become noted for awhile. An editorial in the *Advent Review*, Aug. 19, 1915, says: "In our personal experience we recall at least a dozen during the past two or three decades who have claimed they had the prophetic gift. Two or three of these have drifted into the wildest fantasies. Others frankly acknowledged later in their experience that they had been mistaken, and settled down to a quiet experience. Others are, perhaps, still nursing their fancy."

By this it will be seen that there have been among Seventh-day Adventists right along, numerous persons who *fancied* they had the gift of prophecy. The editor correctly attributes all these to their *fancy*. These had no Elder White to encourage and back them up. So their visions finally ceased, as Mrs. White's in all probability would have done under similar circumstances.

Medical books and cyclopedias, under the words "hysteria,"

"epilepsy," "catalepsy" and "ecstasy," in describing these affections, give a complete description of Mrs. White's cases, as stated by herself, her husband and others. This may be seen from a brief study of these diseases.

1. THE SEX - A FEMALE.

"The vast preponderance of hysteria in the female sex has give rise to its name." (Raynold's "System of Medicine," article "Hysteria".) So say all the authorities. This fits Mrs. White's case.

2. THE AGE.

"Hysteria is infinitely more common among females, beginning usually from fifteen to eighteen or twenty years of age" (*Theory and Practice of Medicine*, by Roberts, p. 399.) "In the female sex, hysteria usually commences at or about the same time of puberty; i.e., between twelve and eighteen years of age." (Raynold's *System of Medicine*, article "Hysteria".)

This again exactly fits the case of Mrs. White. She had her first vision at the age of seventeen. (see *Testimonies*, Vol. I., p. 62.)

"Notwithstanding this mode of life, their health does not materially deteriorate." (*Johnson's Cyclopedia*, article, "Hysteria".) So with Mrs. White. She gradually improved in health and her visions gradually ceased. At first she had visions almost daily, but they grew less frequent as she grew older and healthier, till after about forty-five years of age, from which time she did not average one in five years, and even these were short and light, till she ceased entirely to have them.

Now read this: "Hysteria generally attacks women from the age of puberty to the decline of the peculiar functions of her sex." (*Johnson's Cyclopedia*, article, "Hysteria".) Mrs. White's case again, exactly.

3. THE CAUSE.

Hysteria, epilepsy, catalepsy, and ecstasy are all nervous diseases, which sometimes coexist or alternate or blend together so it is difficult to distinguish them. The causes noted are: "1. Mental disturbance, especially emotional; for example, a sudden fright, prolonged grief or anxiety. 2. Physical influences affecting the brain, as a blow or a fall on the head." (*Theory and Practice of Medicine,* Roberts, p. 393.)

"In ten of my cases the disease was due to reflex causes, which consisted in six cases of injuries to the head." (*Fundamental Nervous Disease*, Putzel, p. 66.)

This fits Mrs. White's case again, exactly. At the age of nine she received a terrible blow on the face, which broke her nose, and nearly killed her. She was unconscious for three weeks. (See her life in *Testimonies*, Vol. I., pp. 9, 10.) This shock to her nervous system was doubtless the chief cause of all the visions she had afterwards.

4. GENERALLY WEAKLY AND SICKLY.

"Most hysterical persons are out of health." (*Theory and Practice of Medicine*, by Roberts, p. 404.) "Fainting fits and palpitations of the heart appear very frequently, and are sometimes so severe that persons affected with them seem to be dying." (*Encyclopedia Americana*, article, "Hysteria".) Now read the life of Mrs. White, and she tells it over and over, times without number, about fainting frequently, pain at the heart, and about being so sick that she expected to die. And it is remarkable that most of her visions were immediately preceded by one of these fainting death spells. This shows plainly that they were the result of nervous weakness.

She says: "My feelings were unusually sensitive." (*Testimonies*, Vol. I., p. 12.) Now read this: "Women...whose nervous system is extremely sensitive are the most subject to hysterical affections." (*Encyclopedia Americana*, article, "Hysteria".) An exact fit.

Philosophy of Her Visions

Mrs. White's Physical Condition as Written by Herself

When Ellen was nine years old, a girl hit her in the face with a stone, which broke her nose and nearly killed her. (*Testimonies for the Church*, Vol. I., p. 9.) "I lay in a stupor for three weeks." (p. 10.) "I was reduced almost to a skeleton." (p. 11.) "My health seemed to be hopelessly impaired." (p. 12.) "My nervous system was prostrated." (p. 13.)

Here was the origin of her hysteria of after years. In this condition she "listened to the starling announcement that Christ was coming in 1843." (p. 14.) "These words kept ringing in my ears: 'The great day of the Lord is at hand.'" (p. 15.) "I frequently attended the meetings and believed that Jesus was soon to come." (p. 22.)

Of her impression of hell she says: "My imagination would be so wrought upon that the perspiration would start." (p. 24.) "I feared that I would lose my reason." (p. 25.) At one time she did become insane for two weeks, as she herself says (*Spiritual Gifts*, Vol. II., p. 51.) She continues: "My health was very poor." (*Testimonies*, Vol. I., p. 55.) It was thought that she could live but a few days.

Then it was she had her first vision, in reality an epileptic fit (p. 58.) "I was but seventeen years of age, small and frail." (p. 62.) "My strength was taken away," and angels talked with her (p. 64.) "My friends thought I could not live...Immediately taken off in vision." (p. 67.)

Notice that her visions occurred when she was very sick! This tells the story; they were the result of her physical weakness. If it was the power of the Holy Ghost, why didn't God send it when she was well? Why not? "I often fainted like one dead." The next day she was well and "rode thirty-eight miles." (p. 80.)

This is characteristic of hysterical persons, as all know who have seen them. They are nearly dying one hour and all well the next. Mrs. White went through that experience a thousand times. She was just dying, was prayed for, was healed by God, and all well in a few minutes. In a few days she went right over it again.

But if God healed her, why didn't she stay healed? This used to bother me. When Jesus healed a man, did he have to go back and be healed again every few days?

She goes on: "I fainted under the burden. Some feared I was dying...I was soon lost to earthly things."–had a vision (p. 86.) Again: "I fainted. Prayer was offered for me, and I was blessed and taken off in vision." (p. 88.)

There is the same old story. It is simply her hysterical imagination, nothing more. Next page: "I fainted...taken off in vision." So she goes on all through her book.

Says the *Encyclopedia Americana*, article "Hysteria": "Fainting fits and palpitation of the heart appear very frequently, and are sometimes so severe that persons afflicted with them seem to be dying." Mrs. White exactly. On page after page the same story is repeated by herself. In the account of her last vision (Jan. 3, 1875), she was very sick till it ended in a vision (*Testimonies*, Vol. III., p. 570.)

Dreadfully sick, almost dead, then a vision–this is the story, times without number, from her own pen. That tells the story. Her visions were the result of her physical weakness.

5. VISIONS IN PUBLIC.

"As a rule, a fit of hysteria occurs when other persons are present, and never comes on during sleep." (*Theory and Practice of Medicine*, by Roberts, p. 401.) Most of Mrs. White's visions occurred in public, and generally while she was very sick, or when praying or speaking earnestly. This was the case with her first vision (*Spiritual Gifts*, Vol. I., p. 30.) So, again, on pages 37, 48, 51, 62, 83, and many more, she had her visions in the presence of many. I do not know that she ever had a vision while alone, or, if so, only once or twice.

6. INCLINATION TO EXAGGERATE AND DECEIVE.

All medical books state that hysterical persons are given to exaggeration and deception. The inclination is irresistible. Nothing can break them of it.

Gurnsey's *Obstetrics*, article, "Hysteria," says: "Such persons entertain their hearers with marvelous tales of the greatness and exploits of their past lives...These accounts are uttered with an air of sincerity well calculated to deceive the honest listener, and such unbridled license of the imagination and total obliviousness in regard to the truth, which are vulgarly attributed to an entire want of principle and the most inordinate vanity, are in reality due to that morbid condition of the female organism which is designated by the comprehensive term 'hysteria.'"

Mrs. White was always telling what great things she had done. The deception which she so often practiced is here accounted for on principles which do not impeach the moral character, and we are glad to accept the explanation.

7. Does Not Breathe.

"Stoppage of respiration usually complete." "Generally appears to hold the breath." (Roberts' *Theory and Practice of Medicine*, p. 393, 394.)

Elder White, describing Mrs. White's condition in vision, says: "She does not breathe." (*Life Incidents*, p. 272.) They always refer to this fact with great confidence as proof of the supernatural in her visions; but it will be seen that it is common in these diseases.

8. Importance Of Self.

"There is a prevailing belief in the importance of self, and the patient thinks that she differs from every other human being." (Raynold's *System of Medicine*, article "Hysteria".)

This was Mrs. White precisely. Hear her laud herself: "It is God, and not an erring mortal, who has spoken." "God has laid upon my husband and myself a special work." "God has appointed us to a more trying work than he has others." (*Testimonies*, Vol. III., pp. 257, 258, 260.) I could prove greater devotion than any one living engaged in the work." (*Testimonies*, Vol. I., p. 581.)

I knew her for nearly thirty years, but I never knew her to

make confession of a single sin in all that time, not one. Seventh-day Adventists ridicule the Pope's claim to infallibility, but they themselves bow to the authority of a woman who made higher claims to infallibility than ever pope or prophet did.

Space will not allow us to fill out every particular of her experience by quotations from medical works compared with her own statements; but those already given are sufficient to show the nature and philosophy of her attacks. They were the result of nervous disease, precisely the same as has often been seen in the case of thousands of other nervous, feeble, and sickly women.

9. TESTIMONY OF PHYSICIANS.

Dr. Fairfield was brought up a Seventh-day Adventist; was for years a physician in their Sanitarium at Battle Creek. He had the best opportunity to observe Mrs. White. He writes:

> Battle Creek, Mich.
> Dec. 28, 1887.
>
> Dear Sir:
>
> You are undoubtedly right in ascribing Mrs. E.G. White's so-called visions to disease. It has been my opportunity to observe her case a good deal, covering quite a period of years, which, with a full knowledge of her history from the beginning, gave me no chance to doubt her ('divine') attacks to be simply hysterical trances. Age itself has almost cured her.
>
> W.J. Fairfield, M.D.

Dr. Wm. Russell, long a Seventh-day Adventist, and a chief physician in the Sanitarium, wrote July 12, 1869, that he had made up his mind some time in the past, "that Mrs. White's visions were the result of a diseased organization or condition of the brain or nervous system."

"When giving, to a conference at Pilot Grove, Ia., 1865, an account of her visit at Dr. Jackson's health institute, she stated that the doctor, upon a medical examination, pronounced her a sub-

PHILOSOPHY OF HER VISIONS

ject of hysteria." (*Mrs. White's Claims Examined*, p. 76.)

This is the testimony of physicians who have personally examined Mrs. White.

At the Sanitarium at Battle Creek, Mich., Mrs. White was often treated when ill. The physicians there became familiar with her case. Several of those most prominent there renounced their faith in her visions. This is significant.

Dr. J.H. Kellogg, for many years the head of that institution, has a world-wide reputation as a physician and a scientist. He was brought up to reverence Mrs. White and her revelations. Through long years he had every opportunity to study her case. Against his best interests he was compelled to lose faith in her visions. He is no longer a believer in her visions.

These physicians, so closely connected with her, learned that the visions were simply the result of her weak physical condition. Mrs. White joined the Millerites in their great excitement of 1843-44. In their meetings she often fainted from excitement. In the enthusiasm and fanaticism of the time many had various "gifts," visions, trances, etc. She drank deeply of their spirit.

The grief and disappointment of the passing of the set time were too much for her feeble condition. Says Dr. Roberts: "The exciting cause of the first hysterical fit is generally some powerful and sudden emotional disturbance."

"Sometimes the attack is preceded by disappointment, fear, violent, exciting, or even religious emotions." (*Library of Universal Knowledge*, article, "Catalepsy".) Just her case, in the great excitement and disappointment of 1844.

In his *Rise and Progress of Seventh-day Adventists*, page 94, Elder J.N. Loughborough gives a description of Mrs. White while having a "vision." Compare it carefully with the condition of patients affected by the diseases already described, many cases of which have been treated by eminent physicians. The two are almost identical, as will be seen.

J.N. LOUGHBOROUGH

Mrs. White's Condition While in Vision

"For about four or five seconds she seems to drop down like a person in a swoon, or one having lost his strength; she then seems to be instantly filled with superhuman strength, sometimes rising at once to her feet and walking about the room. There are frequent movements of the hands and arms, pointing to the right or left as her head turns. All these movements are made in a most graceful manner. In whatever position the hand or arm may be placed, it is impossible for any one to move it. Her eyes are always open, but she does not wink; her head is raised and she is looking upwards, not with a vacant stare, but with a pleasant expression, only differing from the normal in that she appears to be looking intently at some distant object. She does not breathe, yet her pulse beats regularly."

In his *Medical Advisor*, pages 647-650, Dr. H.V. Pierce gives the cause of, and hereditary tendencies to, epilepsy. He says: "Many of the cases treated by us have been brought on as the results of *an injury to the head*. The majority of these forms of disease can be exactly localized in a small area of the brain and may usually be traced to *a blow or fall on the head*."

Of the fit itself, Dr. Pierce says: "It begins suddenly, with little or no warning, commonly with a *cry* or *scream*. In the severe form of the disease, *the respiration is arrested*."

Dr. John Huber, in an article on this subject in the *Washington Post*, June 18, 1916, says that epilepsy is called "the falling sickness" because the patient usually falls over when the paroxysm comes on. He says: "The epileptic fit is a kind of brain storm...The sufferer utters a loud scream at the beginning of the convulsion." These descriptions, written with no reference to Mrs. White, fit her case exactly.

Both of these authorities, it will be noticed, say that the epileptic fit generally begins with a loud cry or scream. This was also characteristic of Mrs. White's "visions." Introducing his description of her condition while in visions, Elder Loughborough, in his work already quoted, same page, says: "*In passing into visions she gives three enraptured shouts of 'Glory!' the second, and especially the third, fainter, but more thrilling than the first.*"

Philosophy of Her Visions

Now read what experienced physicians have written in medical books on trances, ecstasy and catalepsy. Dr. George B. Wood's *Practice of Medicine*, page 721 of Vol. II., in treating of mental disorders and explaining the cause and phenomena of trances, says: "Ecstasy is an affection in which, with a loss of consciousness of existing circumstances, and insensibility to impression from without, there is an apparent exaltation of the intellectual or emotional functions, as if the individual were raised into a different nature, or different sphere of existence. The patient appears wrapped up in some engrossing thought or feeling, with an expression upon his countenance as of lofty contemplations or ineffable delight...Upon recovering from the spell, the patient generally remembers his thoughts and feelings more or less accurately, and sometimes tells of wonderful visions that he has seen, of visits to the regions of the blessed, of ravishing harmony and splendor, of inexpressible enjoyment of the senses or affections."

A person perfectly familiar with Mrs. White could not have described her visions more accurately.

Another high medical authority (G. Durant, M.D., Ph.D., member of the American Medical Association, Fellow of the New York Academy of Medicine, etc., etc., recipient of several medals, etc.), on describing ecstasy and catalepsy, says: "It often happens that the two diseases alternate or coexist. In ecstasy the limbs are motionless, but not rigid. The eyes are open, the pupils fixed, the livid lips parted in smiles, and the arms extended to embrace the beloved vision. The body is erect and raised to its utmost height, or else is extended at full length in recumbent posture. A peculiarly radiant smile illuminates the countenance, and the whole aspect and attitude is that of intense mental exaltation. Sometimes the patient is silent, the mind being apparently absorbed in meditation, or in the contemplation of some beatific vision. Sometimes there is mystical speaking or prophesying, or singing, or the lips maybe moved without any sound escaping...Usually there is complete insensibility to external impressions. Ecstasy is often associated with religious monomania. It was formerly quite common among the inmates of convents, and is now not unfrequently met with at camp meetings and other gatherings of a similar nature. Many truly devout people are ecstatics."

This was Mrs. White's case very clearly. Hundreds of similar ones have occurred in every age and are constantly occurring now. The sad part of it is that so many honest souls are deluded into receiving all this as a divine revelation.

When we remember that Mrs. White's followers, especially during the first ten or fifteen years, were all very common people, wholly unacquainted with such exercises which appeared to them to be miraculous, it is not so strange that they should accept it as the power of God.

She herself was young, uneducated and inexperienced. She could only explain her unusual experiences as miraculous, as the work of the Holy Ghost. So, after doubting awhile, she accepted the view of them. Probably Elder White, at first at least, believed in her visions for the same reason.

All the accounts of her visions which we have were written by her devout believers. We know that they would give only the most favorable aspect of them, omitting anything unfavorable. But, taking their own statements, her symptoms are exactly the same as those described by the physicians as above, where similar visions were merely the results of disease of the nervous system, generally brought on by a blow to the head, as in the case of Mrs. White. Her failures in so many ways, as noted in other chapters of this book, leave no reasonable doubt that the woman was simply deceived herself as to the real nature and cause of her visions.

Mrs. White's visions ceased about the time of the change of life common to women. While she still had visions, she claimed that much that she "saw" went entirely from her mind at the time. Months, even years later, when she met a brother or a church that needed a "testimony," the part relating to these all came vividly to her mind, she said. She would then write out this portion of the forgotten "vision."

This worked very well till years after her visions ceased. Finally this could not be stretched further. Then her revelations had to come in a different way; by a voice, by dreams, by "impressions," by some one on "authority" speaking, and the like.

The following expressions, taken from the last volume of her "Testimonies for the Church," Vol. IX., published in 1909, are examples of this.

Page 13: "I was instructed."

Page 82: "Instruction has been given me."

Page 65: "In the night of March 2, 1907, many things were revealed to me." The room, she said, was very light.

Page 66: "Then a voice spoke to me."

Page 95: "The angel stood by my side." But she had no vision as formerly.

Page 98: "Instruction has been given me."

Page 101: "In the night season I was awakened from a deep sleep and given a view."

Page 137: "In the night season matters have been presented to me."

Page 195: "At one time I seemed to be in a council meeting."

The expression, "I have been instructed," occurs over and over in these later alleged revelations, just as the expression, "I saw," does in her earlier writings. But all this is entirely different from her vision period. Then the Holy Ghost fell on her, her strength was taken away, and she fell to the floor. Then she was carried to heaven, talked with Jesus, visited the planets, and the like.

No such things occurred in her later days. Why this change? The physicians have answered that.

A Great Plagiarist

About 1904, Dr. J.H. Kellogg and his Sanitarium associates, it was learned, were not accepting as from God all of Mrs. White's writings. They found numerous contradictions in them, and believed that many of them were inspired by the officials, and were calling attention to some of these things.

Mrs. White thereupon wrote them a "testimony," asking that they write out their difficulties regarding her writings, and send them to her. In this communication, dated March 30, 1905, she not only promised to clear up these difficulties, but said that God would help her to do this.

She said: "Recently in the visions of the night I stood in a large company of people...I was directed by the Lord to request them, and any others who have perplexities and grievous things in their minds regarding the testimonies that I have borne, to specify what their objections and criticisms are. The Lord will help me to answer these objections, and make plain that which seems to be intricate...Let it all be written out, and submitted to those who desire to remove the perplexities...They should certainly do this, if they are loyal to the directions God has given."

Dr. Charles E. Stewart, one of the Battle Creek Sanitarium physicians, took her at her word, and wrote out a large number of "perplexities" which he and others had found in her writings, and sent them to her. What did Mrs. White do? Instead of fulfilling her promise and attempting an explanation, she had another "vision," in which she was instructed by "a messenger from heaven" not to do so. Here are her words, written under date of June 3, 1906:

"I had a vision, in which I was speaking before a large company, where many questions were asked concerning my work and writings. I was directed by a messenger from heaven not to take the burden of picking up and answering all the sayings and doubts that are being put in many minds."

Notice: First, "in the visions of the night," she was "directed by the Lord" to request those men who had "perplexities and grievous things in their minds" concerning her writings, to "specify what their objections and criticisms are."

"Let it all be written out," she said.

Then she not only promised to answer these objections and criticisms, but said, "The Lord will help me to answer these objections, and make plain that which seems to be intricate."

Then, after the brethren had done exactly what she told them to do, she had another "vision," in which she was "directed by a messenger from heaven" not to do the very thing she promised to do, and said the Lord would help her to do! In doing this she involved herself, and, through claiming divine revelation for what she had written in both communications, involved God, in a most glaring contradiction and cowardly backdown.

As usual, she placed upon God the responsibility for her failure. He had not come to her rescue and helped her as she had said he would, so, through another "vision," she makes him responsible for her breaking her promise.

The simple solution of it all is, she could not clear up these difficulties, nor answer these objections. They were too much for her. Seeking to get these men to commit themselves openly in writing, she had made a promise which she could not fulfill. In the net she had spread for others her own foot was taken. (Ps. 9:15)

One of the perplexities mentioned by Dr. Stewart in his communication was:

THE CHARGE OF PLAGIARISM

The rights of authorship are recognized and protected by copyright laws the world over. Any infringement of these rights, even where credit is given, is punishable by severe penalties, and frequently by confiscation of the works involved.

Plagiarism, or literary piracy, is the worst form of this offense. It is the appropriating of the writings of another as one's own, without quotes or credit. It is indulged in by uneducated, pedantic, and unscrupulous persons, who desire to appear what they are not, or to make money from the products of other minds.

Mrs. White's works abound in offenses of this kind. Few Seventh-day Adventists know this. Many of the striking passages in her writings, which her followers have thought evidences of her inspiration and supernatural powers, have been fond, upon investigation, to have been copied verbatim, or with but slight verbal changes, from the writings of others.

A careful examination has revealed eighteen close parallels between her writings and the Book of Jasher, a book twice mentioned in the Bible, but not a part of the Bible; yet she never once in all her writings refers to the Book of Jasher.

The Standard Dictionary gives the following definition of plagiarism:

> *"The act of plagiarizing or appropriating the ideas, writings or inventions of another without due acknowledgment; especially, the stealing of passages, either word for word or in substance, from the writings of another, and publishing them as one's own; literary or artistic theft."*

One of the damaging facts against the claim of divine revelation in the writings of Mrs. White is that she copied extensively from other authors without giving credit. In the text of her books where she has done this she gives no hint of it in any way. She did not put the passages referred to in quotation marks, nor in any other way indicate that she had made use of the literary productions of others.

The proof of this is abundant in several of her works. In 1883 she published a work, of 334 pages, entitled *Sketches from the Life of Paul*. In the preface the publishers declared it to be written by "special help from the Spirit of God."

In 1855, twenty-eight years prior to this, *The Life and Epistles*

A Great Plagarist

of the Apostle Paul had been published by Conybeare and Howson, two English authors. I have both books. A comparison of them reveals the fact that Mrs. White copied a large part of her book directly from this previously published work. Yet she nowhere makes the least reference to that work, nor does she give credit by the use of quotation marks or otherwise for the material which she thus so extensively copied.

Very few Adventists are aware of this fact; hence they innocently read her book as material given to her by revelation of the Holy Spirit in harmony with the misleading statement made in the preface by the publishers.

In 1907, Dr. Stewart published a pamphlet of eighty-nine pages, in which he arranged in parallel columns quotations from Mrs. White's book and the book by Conybeare and Howson just mentioned. These show beyond dispute that she copied her matter directly from the older book. The material for Dr. Stewart's book was gathered and prepared in response to the request of Mrs. White, in 1905, already referred to. But she never attempted to answer the difficulties he presented. Copies of his book have been in the hands of their leaders now for years; yet not a word of explanation has been attempted.

Dr. Stewart says: "In order to make clear what I mean with reference to the similarity in the two books, I will arrange some of the matter in parallel columns:

Sketches from the Life of Paul By Mrs. E.G. White, 1883.	*Life and Epistles of the Apostle Paul* By Conybeare and Howson, 1855, 3rd ed.
"The judges sat in the open air, upon seats hewn out in the rock, on a platform which was ascended by a flight of stone steps from the valley below." (p. 93)	"The judges sat in the open air, upon seats hewn out in the rock, on a platform which was ascended by a flight of stone steps immediately from the Agora." (p. 308.)
"Had his oration been a direct attack upon their gods, and the great men of the city who where before him, he would have been in danger of meeting the fate of Socrates." (p. 97)	"Had he begun by attacking the national gods in the midst of their sanctuaries, and with the Areopagites on the seats near him, he would have been in almost as great danger as Socrates before him." (p. 310)

"An extensive and profitable business had grown up at Ephesus from the manufacture and sale of these shrines and images." (p. 142)	"From the expressions used by Luke, it is evident that an extensive and lucrative trade grew up at Ephesus from the manufacture and sale of these shrines." (p. 432)
"Only their reverence for the temple saved the apostle from being torn in pieces on the spot. With violent blows and shouts of vindictive triumph, they dragged him from the sacred enclosure." (p. 216)	"It was only their reverence for the Holy Place which preserved him from being torn to pieces on the spot. They hurried him out of the sacred enclosure and assailed him with violent blows." (p. 547)
"In the excitement they flung off their garments as they had done years before at the martyrdom of Stephen and threw dust into the air with frantic violence. This fresh outbreak threw the Roman captain into great perplexity. He had not understood Paul's Hebrew address, and concluded from the general excitement that his prisoner must be guilty of some great crime. The loud demands of the people that Paul be delivered into their hands made the commander tremble. He ordered him to be immediately taken into the barracks and examined by scourging, that he might be forced to confess his guilt." (p. 220)	"In their rage and impatience they tossed off their outer garments (as on that other occasion when the garments were laid at the feet of Saul himself) and threw dust into the air with frantic violence. This commotion threw Lysias into new perplexity. He had not been able to understand the apostle's Hebrew speech and when he saw its results he concluded that his prisoner must be guilty of some enormous crime. He ordered him therefore to be taken immediately from the stairs into the barracks and to be examined by a torture in order to elicit a confession of his guilt." (p. 557)
"Among the disciples who ministered to Paul at Rome was one Onesimus, a fugitive from the city of Colosse. He belonged to a Christian named Philemon, a member of the Colossian church. But he had robbed his master and fled to Rome." (p. 284)	"But all of the disciples now ministering to Paul at Rome, none has for us a greater interest than the fugitive Asiatic slave Onesimus. He belonged to a Christian named Philemon, a member of the Colossian church. But he had robbed his master and at last found his way to Rome." (p. 610)

So plainly and fully was Mrs. White's book copied from the older book, that the publishers of Conybeare and Howson's work threatened prosecution if her work was not suppressed. Hence it was withdrawn from sale, and for many years has not been listed among her books. Did any prophet of old have to suppress one of his books because he had stolen so much of the matter in it from some other writer? The writers of the Bible fre-

A Great Plagarist

quently quote one from the other, but with due credit. (See Dan. 9:1,2; Matt. 24:15; Acts 2:25-28; Rom. 9.)

But, as Dr. Stewart observes, this is not an isolated case. Continuing, he made the following comparisons between her book, *Great Controversy*, and Wylie's *History of the Waldenses* and D'Aubigne's *History of the Reformation*, thus:

Great Controversy By Mrs. E.G. White.	*History of the Waldenses* By Rev. J.A. Wylie.
"The bull invited all Catholics to take up the cross against heretics. In order to stimulate them in this cruel work, it absolved them from all ecclesiastical pains and penalties; it released all who joined the crusade from any oaths they might have taken; it legalized their title to any property which they might have illegally acquired, and promised remission of all their sins to such as should kill any heretic. It annulled all contracts made in favor of the Vaudois, ordered their domestics to abandon them, forbade all persons to give them any aid whatever, and empowered all persons to take possession of their property." (p. 83)	"The bull invited all Catholics to take up the cross against heretics, and to stimulate them in this pious work, it absolved them from all ecclesiastical pains and penalties, general and particular; it released all who joined the crusade from any oaths they might have taken; it legitimatized their title to any property they might have illegally acquired, and promised remission of all their sins to such as should kill any heretic. It annulled all contracts made in favor of the Vaudois, ordered their domestics to abandon them, forbade all persons to give them any aid whatever, and empowered all persons to take possession of their property." (p. 28)

Great Controversy By Mrs. E.G. White.	D'Aubigne's *History of the Reformation*.
"In the gloom of his dungeon, John Huss had foreseen the triumph of true faith. Returning in his dreams to the humble parish where he had preached the gospel, he saw the pope and his bishops effacing the pictures of Christ which he had painted on the walls of his chapel. The sight caused him great distress; but the next day he was filled with joy as he beheld many artists busily engaged in replacing the figures in great numbers and brighter colors. When their work was completed, the painters exclaimed to the immense crowds surrounding them, 'Now let the popes and bishops come! They shall never efface them more!' Said the reformer as he related his dream, 'I	"One night the holy martyr saw, in imagination, from the depths of his dungeon, the pictures of Christ that he had painted on the walls of his oratory, effaced by the popes and his bishops. The vision distressed him; but on the next day he saw many painters occupied in restoring these figures in greater numbers and in brighter colors. As soon as their task was ended, the painters, who were surrounded by an immense crowd, exclaimed, 'Now let the popes and bishops come! They shall never efface them more!' ...'I am no dreamer,' replied Huss, 'but I maintain this for certain: That the image of Christ will never be effaced. They have wished to destroy it, but it

am certain that the image of Christ will never be effaced. They have wished to destroy it, but it shall be painted in all hearts by much better preachers than myself.'" (pp. 91, 92)

shall be painted afresh in all hearts by much better preachers than myself.'" (p. 3)

Here are other examples of Mrs. White's plagiarisms:

Unpublished Testimony of Mrs. White, Aug 5, 1896:

"The laws governing the physical nature are as truly divine in their origin and character as the law of the ten commandments." *Testimony*, **Vol. II**. "It is just as much a sin to violate the law of our being as to break on of the ten commandments." (p. 70.)

Cole's *Philosophy of Health*, Published 1853, 26th ed.

"The laws which govern our constitutions are divine; and to their violation there is affixed a penalty, which must sooner or later be met. And it is as truly a sin to violate one of these laws as it is to violate one of the ten commandments." (p. 8.)

Mrs. White's *Great Controversy* ed. 1888.

"The cross of Christ will be the science and the song of the redeemed through all eternity." (p. 651.)

Robert Pollok's *Course of Time*, written in 1829.

"Redemption is the science and the song of all eternity." (p. 55)

These quotations from her different books show that Mrs. White practiced this literary stealing right along all through her life. Ten times as much could readily be given.

The Great Controversy is her most popular book with her people. Every line is accepted as original with her; all inspired by the Holy Spirit. Carefully studying it, we found that it was largely taken from Andrews' *History of the Sabbath*, Wylie's *History of the Waldenses*, D'Aubigne's *History of the Reformation*, Smith's *Sanctuary*, Elder White's *Life of Wm. Miller*, itself a copied book, and other works.

The quotations already given are sufficient to show that Mrs. White's inspiration was from very human sources, although she sent her works forth as inspired by the Holy Spirit. The facts here cited are all in print, and can not successfully be denied. From these facts the reader can judge for himself as to how much reliance can be placed on her claim that all her writings were inspired and dictated by the Holy Spirit.

In his communication to her Dr. Stewart said: "I am informed by a trustworthy person who has had an opportunity to know, that you, in the preparation of your various works, consulted freely other authors; and that it was sometimes very difficult to arrange the matter for your books in such a way as to prevent the reader from detecting that many of the ideas had been taken from other authors."

Remember that Mrs. White never answered Dr. Stewart's communication, which she herself invited through her professed revelation from God on March 30, 1905. And since she did not in several years find it either possible or convenient to answer what she had not only promised to answer, but what she said God would help her to answer, it is evident that it is impossible for these objections to be answered. Mrs. White can not answer them now, for she is dead; and after a lapse of more than eleven years none of her followers has attempted to answer them.

One Advent sister who had been with Mrs. White for ten years told the author personally that she had seen her copying from a book in her lap. When visitors came in she would cover the book with her apron until they had gone, then proceed with her copying. Her works show that the sister told the truth.

Such work is considered dishonorable in anyone. It is defined as "literary theft." Webster says:

> "Plagiarist: A thief in literature; one who purloins another's writings and offers them to the public as his own."

This is exactly what Mrs. White did, as already shown. But she did more than steal her material from other authors; she sent it forth to the world as a divine revelation given to her by the Holy Spirit from God himself.

Occasionally a college student is detected in the appropriation from some author of an essay which he submits to his teacher as his own production. When discovered, he is promptly expelled or suspended for misconduct.

As may be seen from the preface or introduction to almost any standard or reputable work, honorable authors take pleasure in acknowledging the assistance they have received from the productions or labors of others. Mrs. White, it seems, suppressed this fact as far as possible in the preparation and publication of her works.

The only plausible excuse that can be offered for this is that she had a diseased brain, and was a monomaniac on the subject of her visions, revelations and religious ideas, and thought her "gift" gave her a right to do that which would be reprehensible in others. This accounts for her numerous plagiarisms and contradictions, which never seemed to trouble her.

Had we the space, we could give dates, places, and names of persons involved, when we, with others, told her all about certain circumstances having to do with some other persons; shortly, she would have a "testimony" for them respecting what we had told her; but, instead of telling the source of her information, she delivered it as a direct revelation from God. She knew that we were aware of the source of her information; but that did not seem to disconcert her at all.

All of those near to her well understood how to use her influence through testimonies, and many of them did it. Especially did her husband, Elder White, secure in this way "divine sanction" for all his plans. It helped him in a remarkable way, as it did also her two sons and other leaders later.

Therefore, neither he nor they would allow Mrs. White's "revelations" to be questioned in any way. To do so was the greatest of all heresies, and meant summary excommunication from the church, without hearing or trial.

In 1909, at the last General Conference of her people that Mrs. White ever attended, a glaring illustration of her plagiarism was discovered. A certain minister was asked to read one morning before a large audience, a selection from a collection of her unpublished testimonies. As he read it he recognized it as his own production. Without quotes or credit of any kind, Mrs. White had taken it bodily from a communication which he had sent her some years before, and appropriated it as her own.

This man, who from childhood had been taught to believe in

A Great Plagarist

her inspiration, was dumbfounded, and began to investigate her claims for himself. To his surprise, he soon found them groundless.

Miss Marian Davis, the literary worker who had the most to do of any one in the preparation of Mrs. White's books, was one day heard moaning in her room. Going in, another worker inquired the cause of her trouble. Miss Davis replied: "I wish I could die! I wish I could die!"

"Why, what is the matter?" asked the other.

"Oh" Miss Davis said, "this terrible plagiarism!"

It is said that before her death Miss Davis was greatly troubled over the connection she had had with Mrs. White's plagiarism, for she knew how extensively it had been carried on.

In 1911, only four years before Mrs. White's death, three thousand dollars was spent on the revision of her book, *Great Controversy*, chiefly to relieve it of some of its most glaring plagiarisms. The revision began to be demanded by some of her own people who had become aware of the facts.

This charge against her, therefore, must stand. She was a copyist rather than an original or inspired writer. While professing to be the special mouthpiece for God, she was guilty of practicing this literary fraud practically all her life. This nullifies her claim to inspiration. God does not inspire his prophets to steal.

While Mrs. White took so freely from the writings of others without giving credit, and thus took credit to herself which did not belong to her, she was very particular about receiving credit herself.

Jan. 30, 1905, Dr. David Paulson, of Chicago, wrote her, asking permission to make extracts from her writings for his monthly magazine, *The Life-boat*. Feb. 15, 1905, her son, W.C. White, replied as follows:

> "Mother instructs me to say to you that you may be free to select from her writings short articles for The Life-boat. Or you may make extracts from these MSS. and from similar writings, in your articles, in each case giving the proper credit."

Why did not Mrs. White do as she wished to be done by, and

"in each case," where she made use of the writings of others, give "the proper credit"?

From what has been presented, the answer is plain. She was so anxious to make books, so possessed with the idea of her own self-importance, and so desirous of appearing something she was not, that she ignored the rights of others, purloined from their writings, and became a pronounced literary kleptomaniac.

W.C. WHITE

Used Her Gift to Get Money

There is no example in the Bible where a prophet took advantage of his inspiration to enrich himself. The prophets of the Bible generally worked hard, had little, and died poor.

Mrs. White and her husband began poor. She says: "We entered upon our work penniless." (*Testimonies*, Vol. I., p. 75.) But as soon as they became leaders, they commercialized their work, and managed to supply themselves well. They soon had abundance, and used means for themselves lavishly. They would always have the best of everything, and plenty of it. Everywhere they went they required to be waited upon in the most slavish manner.

At an early campmeeting in Michigan they sent their son Edson out in camp crying: "Who has a chicken for mother? Mother wants a chicken."

Mrs. White dressed richly, and generally had a number of attendants to wait on her. When Elder White died, it is said he left some $15,000 or $20,000. He took advantage of his position to benefit himself and family financially, and she aided him by her revelations.

She received a larger salary than was paid most of the ministers of the denomination; received pay for all her articles furnished to the leading papers of the denomination (while others generally contributed theirs gratuitously); besides receiving a large and increasing income from the royalties on all her books. For several years before she died, because of the "peculiar position" she occupied in the church, she was paid a higher royalty than was paid other authors in the denomination.

Take an example of how she used her revelations to make

money: In 1868, Elder White had on hand several thousand dollars' worth of old books which were dead property, as they were not selling, and were going out of date. He hit on a plan to raise a "book fund" for the free distribution of books and tracts. This fund he used to buy out his and his wife's old books.

When the money did not come fast enough, she had a revelation about it thus: "Why do not our brethren send in their pledges on the book and tract fund more liberally? And why do not our ministers take hold of this work in earnest?...We shall not hold our peace upon this subject. Our people will come up to the work. The means will come. And we would say to those who are poor and want books, send in your orders...We will send you a package containing four volumes of *Spiritual Gifts, How to Live, Appeal to Youth, Appeal to Mothers, Sabbath Readings,* and two large charts, with key of explanation,...and charge the fund four dollars." (*Testimonies*, Vol. I., p. 689.)

Every one of these books was their own. The money came, and they pocketed it all. I was there, and know.

Mrs. White had about twenty inspired books. To sell these, every possible effort has been made through every channel. She was constantly urging their sale by all her inspired authority. Hear her: "The volume of *Spirit of Prophecy* and also the *Testimonies* should be introduced into every Sabbath-keeping family...Let them be worn out in being read by all the neighbors...Prevail upon them to buy copies...Light so precious, coming from the throne of God, is hid under a bushel. God will make his people responsible for this neglect." (*Testimonies*, Vol. IV., pp. 390, 391.)

See how she lauds her own books! So, of course, her books were pushed and sold in large numbers, and as a result she received large financial returns. Her royalties from only one of their publishing houses (the one located in Washington, D.C.), in 1911, amounted to over $8,000, or more than the net profits of the house itself that year. From one book alone she received over $4,000 royalty, and from all of her books over $100,000.

In his book *Past, Present and Future*, page 367, edition 1909, her son, Edson White, accuses Mrs. Eddy of "simony" because she took advantage of her system to make money. The charge lays equally against Mrs. White. If one practiced simony, so did the other.

Mrs. White herself, however, was not a good business manager. She advised the brethren to undertake several business projects which proved great financial failures.

June 8, 1905, she wrote Elder W.J. Fitzgerald, president of the East Pennsylvania Conference, to "go right forward" in the purchase of a certain building in Philadelphia for a sanitarium; "raise every penny possible." He did so. The institution proved a failure, was finally closed, and the building sold at a loss of over $60,000 to the denomination.

About the same time she gave similar instruction regarding the purchase of another building for a sanitarium at Nashville, Tenn. This was likewise a failure, and entailed a loss of $30,000.

A little later, through her advice, the denomination was plunged into over $400,000 debt at Loma Linda, Cal., although in 1901 she had told her followers to "shun the incurring of debt as you would shun disease," and that "we should shun debt as we would shun leprosy." (*Testimonies*, Vol. VI., pp. 211, 217.) Her conflicting instruction threw the leaders into great perplexity.

Not long after her husband's death she became financially embarrassed, notwithstanding her large income. For many years she kept such a retinue of servants that her family expenses were heavy. When she died she is said to have been heavily in debt, although owning a large home and a ranch in California, worth probably $20,000, besides the plates and copyrights to her numerous books, worth many thousands more. To save her credit, the General Conference assumed her obligations.

Mrs. White gave very explicit instruction about the duty of publishing houses paying royalty to authors (see *Testimonies*, Vol. V., pp. 563-566.) Contrary to her plain instructions, however, the denominational leaders are planning to discontinue, as far as possible, the paying of royalty altogether. The example she set in this matter seems to have turned them against it, and led them to disregard both her plain instructions and the rights of authors.

Her High Claims Disproved

No prophet of God ever made stronger claims than did Mrs. White. In *Spiritual Gifts*, Vol. II., page 293, she says: "I am just as dependent upon the Spirit of the Lord in relating or writing a vision as in having a vision."

Here she claims that the very words in which her visions are recorded are of divine inspiration. But I know that the words in her books and written "testimonies" are not inspired; for:

1. She often changed what she had written, and wrote it very differently. I have seen her scratch out a line, a sentence, and even a whole page, and write it over differently. If Go gave her the words, why did she scratch them out and alter them? Does God change his mind that way?

2. I have seen her sit with pen in hand and read her manuscript to her husband, while he suggested changes, which she made. She would scratch out her own words and put in his. Was he inspired too?

She denied this. In *Testimonies*, Vol. I., page 612, she says: "I have never regarded his judgment as infallible, nor his words inspired." And yet in preparing her writings she would take his words in preference to her own.

3. As she was ignorant of grammar, she employed accomplished writers to take her manuscript and correct it, improve its wording, polish it up, and put it in popular style, so her books would sell better. Thousands of words, phrases and sen-

tences, not her own, were thus put in by these other persons, some of whom were not even Christians. Were their words inspired too?

4. One of her employees worked for over eight years preparing her largest book. After completing it, she said: "I got a little here, and a little there, and a little somewhere else, and wove it all together."

The manager of one of their largest publishing houses, who was intimately acquainted with her work, said that he did not suppose that Mrs. White ever prepared a whole chapter for one of her popular subscription books. They were all the work of others.

5. In gathering matter for her books Mrs. White often copied her subject matter, without credit or sign of quotation, from other authors, none of whom claimed divine inspiration for their writings. See the chapter on her plagiarisms. Were these authors inspired?

6. Many of the things which she says "I saw," "I was shown," "I have been shown," are now known to be false. These expressions abound in her writings for the church. In the one small book, *Early Writings,* they occur 409 times. But God does not show his prophets things which are not true. Therefore God did not show her what she claims he did.

7. The denominational leaders often treated her writings as they would any ordinary literary production, and not as the inspired word of God. Here is the testimony of one who knows:

> "This is to certify that I was proof-reader in the *Review and Herald* office here for six years, beginning in 1898. Many times when testimonies from Mrs. White were received, passages were cut out and left out as it suited those in authority in the office."
>
> (Signed) W.R. Vester

On Oct. 7, 1907, at Battle Creek, Mich., a church committee called on Dr. J.H. Kellogg to inquire into his religious views, especially his attitude toward the testimonies of Mrs. White. The interview lasted eight hours, from 8:30 A.M. till 4:30 P.M., was stenographically reported, and covered 164 typewritten pages.

The doctor allowed that Mrs. White meant to be a Christian woman, but held that her testimonies were not reliable. He gave many instances where she contradicted well known facts–contradicted what she herself had written, and denied what she had said. He gave many instances where officials had simply used her to get testimonies to suit their projects. He gave instances where these officials had cut out of her testimonies parts they did not like, put other pieces together to change the meaning, and then, with her name signed, used them to further their schemes, and "down" men they wished to silence.

On page 48 of this report the doctor says: "These men have frequently cut out large chunks of things that Sister White had written, that put things in a light that was not the most favorable to them, or did not suit their campaigns that way; they felt at liberty to cut them out so as to change the effect and the tenor of the whole thing, sending it out over Sister White's name. I know that, and I think you know it too."

The committee could not contradict him. This shows how little respect the officials have for the testimonies.

On page 51 the doctor says: "I do not believe in Mrs. White's infallibility, and never did. I told her eight years ago, to her face, that some of the things she had sent me as testimonies were not the truth, that they were not in harmony with facts; and she herself found it out." She finally confessed to him, he said, that she had been mistaken.

On page 96 he says again: "I know that fraud is being perpetrated right along, and I have no sympathy with that at all. I know that people go to Sister White with some plan or scheme they want to carry through under her endorsement of it, and stand up and say, 'The Lord has spoken!'" In fact, that is the way a large share of her "testimonies" were given; that is, through the influence of someone over her, to write what he wanted written.

On page 62, G.W. Amadon, for many years head printer in the *Review* office, and a member of the committee who examined Dr. Kellogg, said: "You know, in the days of the Elder [Elder James White], how her writings were handled, just as well as I do."

Dr. Kellogg replied: "Of course I do." That is, Elder White manipulated them to suit himself. Later, others did the same thing.

On page 130 the doctor says Mrs. White said to him: "Dr. Kellogg, I sometimes doubt my own experience." That was in 1881. This shows that all along, at times, she was not sure that her visions were of God.

On the same page the doctor says that Elder White came to him one day and said: "Dr. Kellogg, it is wonderful; my wife sometimes has the most remarkable experiences; the Lord comes near her and she has the most remarkable experiences; and then again the very devil comes in and takes possession of her." These statements throw some remarkable sidelights on the life of Mrs. White, and give additional proof that she was not inspired.

8. She herself suppressed some of her own writings, for which, at the time of their first publication, she claimed divine inspiration. See the chapter on "Damaging Writings Suppressed."

9. Lastly, in the revision of some of her books she directly contradicts what she had previously written. Thus, in all editions of her book, *Great Controversy*, page 383, from 1888 up to 1911, of the fall of Babylon referred to in Rev. 14:8, she said: "It can not refer to the Romish Church." She applied it altogether to the Protestant churches.

But in the revised edition of 1911, this statement was changed to read: "It can not refer to the Romish Church alone." Before this it could not refer to the Roman Church at all; but now she says it does apply to that church, and to that church particularly, but not to it alone. It includes others.

Here is a direct contradiction if ever there was one. What, then, becomes of her claim to divine inspiration for her writings, and to the still more presumptuous claim of her followers that her writings are "the only infallible interpreter" of the Bible? Does God change his mind and contradict himself in that way?

The foregoing chapters have clearly shown the real source of her inspiration.

First Visions Childish

The ideas, and the way of expressing them, in her first visions are often crude, childish, and extravagant, differing in this, materially, from her writings in later years. At the time of her first visions she was only seventeen, unread, and filled with the fanatical ideas of the Millerites of that date. These visions were in keeping with her surroundings and her childish mind at that time.

In her first vision she says she saw "a tree with a trunk on either side of the river, both of pure, transparent gold." (*Early Writings*, edition 1907, p. 17.) Again: "I saw two long rods on which hung silver wires, and on the wires most glorious grapes."

Think of a fruit tree of gold, and of silver wires bearing grapes! A worthy idea for a childish mind.

Once again: "All the angels hold a golden card, which they must present at the gate of the holy city, to get in and out." (p. 39.)

Every saint of all the untold millions saved has a crown of gold. She says: "Jesus with his own right hand placed them on our heads." (p. 16.) For Jesus himself to do all this for all the myriads of the redeemed, would require hundreds of years.

Then she sees "a table of pure silver; it was many miles in length, yet our eyes could extend over it." (p. 19.)

The saints all have silver houses; in each house is a shelf of gold. The saints take off their golden crowns, lay them on the shelf, and go out to work in the ground. (p. 18.)

She sees little children "use their little wings and fly to the top of the mountains." (p. 19.) Again: "The saints used their wings and mounted to the top of the wall." (p. 53.)

Where is the Scripture for such teaching? She claimed to have had a minute view of Satan; saw his frame, shape of his head, his eyes, etc. She says: "His frame was large, but the flesh hung loosely about his hands and face. As I beheld him, his chin was resting upon his left hand." (p. 152.)

Notice her extreme, materialistic views of everything like a simple-minded, imaginative child, just what she really was at that time. In her later writings, when she became more intelligent and better read, these crude ideas largely disappear.

Her ideas of the fall of Satan, the fall of man, and the loss of Eden look as if she got them from Milton's *Paradise Lost*, surely not from the Bible.

Look at her views regarding the destruction of the wicked. She says some were consumed "quickly." "Some were many days consuming, and just as long as there was a portion of them unconsumed, all the sense of suffering remained." (p. 294; old edition, p. 154.) So if a thigh bone was the last to burn after the brain and all the nerves were gone, that bone could think and feel and understand, and suffer, without head or brain! This is worthy of Dante's Inferno, or the old medieval idea of torture in literal fire. God would have to work a miracle in each individual case to torture men that way.

While Dr. Kellogg was in her high favor, Mrs. White used the most extravagant terms in his praise. Here is one instance: Dr. Kellogg "took up the most difficult cases, where, if the knife had slipped one hair's-breadth, it would have cost a life. God stood by his side and an angel's hand was upon his hand, guiding it through operations." (General Conference Bulletin, 1901, p. 203.)

If an angel could do this for Dr. Kellogg, other angels could do the same for any devout surgeon, or even for a person who never studied surgery at all. This illustrates the ungoverned bridle upon her fertile imagination in all her writings.

In 1901 she called Dr. Kellogg "God's appointed physician." A little later (July 23, 1904) she denounced him as a tool of the devil, and said he had been "taught by the master of sophistries" (*Special Testimonies*, Series B, p. 43.)

First Visions Childish

A Historical Blunder About the Two Herods

In her early years, especially, Mrs. White was entirely ignorant of history. Hence she made many mistakes which are very apparent. Here is one about the two Herods:

One Herod took part in the trial of Christ; years later another Herod put James to death. Mrs. White did not know this, but supposed it was the same Herod in both cases. So this is her inspired comment: "Herod's heart grew still harder; and when he heard that Christ was risen, he was not much troubled. He took the life of James," etc. (*Early Writings*, second part, p. 54.)

A note by the publisher, at the bottom of this page, makes this confession: "It was Herod Antipas who took part in the trial of Christ, and Herod Agrippa who put James to death." And they try to fix matters up for her by saying: "It was the same Herodian spirit, only in another personality."

Did not the Lord know the difference between the two Herods? Surely!

Did he inspire Mrs. White to write this false statement? No.

The simple fact is, she wrote this out of her own mind as she supposed it was. It affords clear proof that she was not inspired.

Editor Smith Rejected Her Testimonies

Uriah Smith was editor of the *Review and Herald*, their church paper, for over fifty years. All these years he was intimately associated with Mrs. White, and had every possible opportunity to judge of her claims to divine inspiration.

Like most of us, he began with the fullest confidence in her claims. In 1868 he wrote a lengthy defense of her visions, in a pamphlet of 144 pages. As the years went by he began to question her inspiration.

First, he denied that the "testimony of Jesus" of Rev. 12:17 meant to prophesy and be a prophet, as Mrs. White assumed. His position on this was well known. Later he argued that we must discriminate between a direct "vision" and simply letter, or testimonies, she wrote.

From Healdsburg, Cal., March 28, 1882, Mrs. White wrote Elder Smith a scathing letter, condemning him, and requiring him to read what she had written him to the church at Battle Creek. This he refused to do. He said it was only a letter giving her personal opinion, and was not inspired. It cut him deeply.

June 20, 1882, she wrote a letter to the church saying she had written Smith, and that he had withheld the testimony. Both of these communications he was compelled to have printed in *Testimonies for the Church*, No. 31, pages 41-80; the first under the heading, "Important Testimony," and the second under the caption, "The Testimonies Slighted." Then these were circulated through all the churches everywhere.

This was humiliating to Smith; but he had to swallow it or

rebel. For years it was a question which he would do.

In the first letter Mrs. White said: "You despise and reject the testimonies" (p. 45.) Here Mrs. White, in an inspired revelation, testifies that Smith had rejected the testimonies. So it must stand as a fact, which he never denied.

In the second she said: "If you lessen the confidence of God's people in the testimonies he has sent them, you are rebelling against God as certainly as were Korah, Dathan and Abiram...God was speaking through clay." (pp. 62, 63.)

Believing, with others, that Smith was about to rebel, she said: "In the mighty sifting soon to take place...many a star that we have admired for its brilliancy, will then go out in darkness." (pp. 76, 77.)

But the prediction failed. The "mighty sifting soon to take place" did not occur, nor has it occurred during the thirty-five years since the prediction was made, and Smith, though doubting, remained in the church.

In the second letter, Mrs. White said: "You might say that this communication was only a letter. Yes, it was a letter, but prompted by the Spirit of God." (p. 63.)

Smith yielded, but was not convinced. It only increased his doubts. He talked them freely to me. One day on the steps of the Battle Creek Tabernacle I said to him: "You have written a defense of the visions; but it is not satisfactory to yourself." He simply laughed.

BATTLE CREEK TABERNACLE

I laid one finger across another and said: "You know they contradict themselves just like that." Again he laughed and said nothing.

Apr. 6, 1883, Elder Smith wrote me thus: "If the visions should drop out entirely, it would not affect my faith in our Biblical theories at all...I did not learn any of these things from the visions...The idea has been studiously instilled into the minds of the people that to question the visions in the least is to become at once a hopeless apostate and rebel."

July 31, 1883, he wrote me again: "Sister White herself has shut my mouth. In the special testimony to the Battle Creek Church she has published me as having rejected, not only that testimony, but *all* the testimonies. Now, if I say I haven't rejected them, I thereby show that I have, for I contradict this one. But if I say I have, that will not do them any good." Poor fellow, he was indeed in a dilemma.

Under date of Aug. 7, 1883, he wrote me once again: "I now have to discriminate between 'testimony' and 'vision.' I think I know myself as well as Sister White knows me."

March 22, 1883, he again wrote me: "It seems to me that the testimonies have practically come into that shape that it is not any use to try to defend the enormous claims that are now put forth for them. At least, after the unjust treatment I have received the past year, I feel no burden in that direction."

Oct. 2, 1883, he wrote me that he allowed it to be understood that he had not rejected the testimonies, lest others by his example should be led to give up, not only the testimonies, but all the rest of the message as well. With this plausible excuse he silenced his conscience, allowed his influence to favor what he did not himself believe, and kept his office. From this it will be seen that he was compelled to live a double life, as many other high officials in that church all along have done and are now doing. Publicly, Smith accepted the testimonies; privately, he did not believe them.

When I left the Adventists, I stated that Elder Smith, like myself, doubted the testimonies. The officials then pressed him to state in the *Review* his position regarding them. This put him in a tight place.

After much pressure, he wrote a short article headed "Personal." Every line of this shows that he tried to say something without really saying anything.

His brethren were not satisfied. I was told he said, "You will take that or nothing."

Here are a few lines from his statement:

> "Just how near I ever did come to giving them up, I am willing any one should know who wishes to know if it can be determined. Perhaps I have not come so near as some suppose; perhaps not so near as I have supposed myself...Under what has seemed, for the time, strong provocations to withdraw from the work, I have canvassed the question how far this could reasonably be done, or how much of this work could consistently be surrendered...A little reflection is sufficient to show that the message, and that which has accompanied it, can not be separated. Well, then, says one, the absurdity of this part [the visions] of the work is sufficient to overthrow the other. To which I reply, No, for the strength of the other parts is sufficient to hold a person from giving up this. And this has been the position I have occupied."*

Here Smith owns that Mrs. White's visions are absurd, and that, standing by themselves, he would have given them up. It was his faith in the other parts of the message which held him from repudiating them. And this is what he told me

---

* *Replies to Canright*, p. 108

personally.

In the testimonies themselves he saw no evidence of divine inspiration, but he did see enough against them to reject them as absurd. No man ever had a better chance to know this than he. For the last thirty years of his life he reluctantly outwardly accepted the testimonies, because he had to or be ousted from office.

He was a fair illustration of the spiritual bondage in which many of their more intelligent ministers and officials are held now. I myself wore that galling yoke for years, and know what it means.

Once, Elder W.C. Gage, another prominent Adventist minister, said to me: "I hate and despise myself for pretending to believe what I do not believe;" that is, the testimonies. Yet, like Elder Smith, he swallowed his doubts, smothered his conscience, and stayed there till his death, as many more are doing now.

Her Prophecies Fail

Mrs. White and her followers claim that she had the "spirit of prophecy" from December, 1844, to the end of her life, August, 1915–seventy-one years. During these long years she wrote over twenty volumes. All this time she claimed that the future was being revealed to her, and predicted what would happen.

Here her claims can be examined and tested.

God's prophets foretold definite things to occur; named persons and cities, and told what would happen to each, and when.

Joseph foretold the seven years of plenty and seven years of famine. (Gen. 41.)

Samuel told Saul that the kingdom would be taken from him and given to another. (1 Sam. 15:28.)

Isaiah named Cyrus two hundred years before he was born. (Isa. 44:28.)

Jeremiah foretold the fall of Babylon. (Jer. 51.)

Daniel prophesied regarding the rise and fall of Babylon, Medo-Persia, Greece and Rome. (Dan. 2 and 7.)

Jesus warned of the destruction of Jerusalem. (Matt. 24.)

Agabus foretold what would happen to Paul at Jerusalem. (Acts 21:10, 11.)

Scores of such cases could be given. But where are the fulfilled predictions of Mrs. White during her seventy-one years of prophesying? What definite events did she foretell to occur at definite times and to definite cites? Where are these prophecies?

Nowhere in all her numerous volumes.

At first, she did venture to foretell a few things definitely, but they all failed. After, she invariably put everything in general terms, not venturing to name definitely any persons or cities or places or time. She predicted numerous floods, storms, earthquakes, wars, etc., all in general terms. Anyone could do that safely, without any prophetic gift.

If she really had the spirit of prophecy, that should have been the outstanding feature of her books. Instead of this, her *Testimonies* and other books are devoted almost wholly to personal matters, expositions of the Bible, and to practical subjects regarding Christian conduct and duty, the same as any intelligent religious teacher could write.

Once in her early work she did venture to predict the curse of God upon a definite person, Moses Hull. In 1862 he was about to give up his faith in Adventism. Mrs. White wrote him thus: "If you proceed in the way you have started, misery and woe are before you. God's hand will arrest you in a manner that will not suit you. His wrath will not slumber." (*Testimonies for the Church,* Vol. I., pp. 430, 431.)

Mr. Hull lived on many long years to a ripe old age, and nothing of the kind predicted happened. After this, she threatened many, but always in general terms.

PREDICTIONS ABOUT THE CIVIL WAR

The Civil War of 1861-65 placed Seventh-day Adventists in a trying position. They could not engage in war and keep the Sabbath. The draft threatened them. Now, what?

I was one of them, twenty years old–the right age to go to war. So I remember it all distinctly. Something had to be done.

We hoped Mrs. White would have a revelation. And she did have–several of them, covering thirty pages of printed matter in Volume I. of *Testimonies for the Church.* At the time, we read these revelations with great anxiety, hoping for light ahead. We were disappointed. They simply told just what everybody already knew, reflecting the sentiments of those opposed to the Government and the war. It was a forced attempt to say something when she had nothing to tell.

Read in the light of today, it is seen to be mere guess work, mostly wrong. She says, "It was necessary that something be

Her Prophecies Fail

said" (*Testimonies*, Vol. I., p. 356.) It was all directed to us, a little handful of about ten thousand, half women, none of any influence in the Government or in the war. Bible prophets went directly to the king and told him how to conduct the war, and what the end would be. Our prophet had no such message.

She says: "Jan. 4, 1862, I was shown some things in regard to our nation." (p. 253.) It is all a bitter denunciation of Lincoln's administration and his management of the war. Every move had been wrong, and only defeat was prophesied. But the verdict of history is that Lincoln was one of the wisest and most successful men who ever led a nation through a crisis. The whole world honors him. With the most tremendous odds against him on the start, he conducted the war to a glorious victory, preserved the union, freed the slaves, and benefited even the South.

During the dark hours of that awful struggle, how he needed the encouragement of a prophet of God, if there was one, as Mrs. White claimed to be. But her whole message was one of opposition, faultfinding, condemnation, and a prophecy of defeat and final failure–exactly that of the opponents of Lincoln and his management of the war.

Listen to her: "The rebellion was handled so carefully, so slowly, that many...joined the Southern Confederacy who would not, had prompt and thorough measures been carried out by our Government at an early period...How little has been gained! Thousands have been induced to enlist with the understanding that this war was to exterminate slavery; but now that they are fixed, they find that they have been deceived; that the object of this war is not to abolish slavery, but to preserve it as it is." "The war is not to do away with slavery, but merely to preserve the Union." (pp. 254, 258.)

This was only a few months after the war began. Like her, some unwise hot-heads urged Lincoln to immediately declare slavery abolished. General Fremont had to be removed from his command because he began that very thing in the West. It was premature. The general sentiment of the nation was not ready for it. Lincoln only waited and watched for the proper time. Then it was a success. Now all see the wisdom of his course.

Mrs. White goes on: "They [the soldiers] inquire, 'If we succeed in quelling the rebellion, what has been gained?' They can only answer discouragingly, 'Nothing.'" (p. 255.)

Fine language to encourage Mr. Lincoln, the soldiers and the North in the dark hour of their need! She continues: "The system of slavery, which has ruined our nation, is left to live and stir up another rebellion." (same page.)

A plain, false prophecy. No such thing happened, as all now know.

Again: "The prospects before our nation are discouraging." (same page.) Yes, as far as humans could see. But she claimed to have divine revelations of the future. Had her claim been true, she would have seen the victory at the end, disproving her words.

Hear her again in the same gloomy tone: "As this war was shown to me, it looked like the most singular and uncertain that has ever occurred...It seems impossible to have the war conducted successfully." (p. 256.)

Yes, to her it was uncertain, impossible to succeed. But was that all God knew about? All he could tell her? Remember, she is writing by God's inspiration; writing the words he tells her! Everything she writes, whether in a private letter or newspaper article, she says, is inspired. Thus: "God was speaking through clay...In these letters which I write, in the testimonies I bear, I am presenting to you that which the Lord has presented to me. I do not write one article in the paper, expressing merely my own ideas. They are what God has opened before me in vision - the precious rays of light shining from the throne." ("Testimonies," Vol. V., p. 67.)

There you have it, Simon-pure–every word she writes is a ray of light from the throne of God! So, to God it was an uncertain war, impossible to succeed! So the Lord must have been greatly surprised when it did really succeed!

Mr. Lincoln, in his need, asked the prayers of all Christians, and appointed days of fasting and prayer. Of these Mrs. White said: "I saw that these national fasts were an insult to Jehovah...A national fast is proclaimed! Oh, what an insult to Jehovah!" (*Testimonies,* Vol. I., p. 257.) That was the way she sympathized with Mr. Lincoln and the nation in the hour of need.

A day before the awful battle of Gettysburg, on which the destiny of the nation would turn, Mr. Lincoln spent the night in agonizing prayer to almighty God. So his biographer testifies. But neither Mrs. White nor any of her followers offered a single prayer for him or the nation. I was with her–and with them–and know.

During the entire twenty-eight years I was an Adventist I never offered one prayer for the President, for Congress, for a Governor, or any one in authority. I never heard Mrs. White, Elder White, or any one of them, do it. I have often attended their large meetings since then, but never heard a prayer offered for any Government official. Yet one of the plainest commands of the gospel is that we should pray for kings, rulers and all in authority. (1 Tim. 2:1, 2.)

Since Mrs. White died, Adventists have begun to pray for Government officials.

Again Mrs. White said: "This nation will yet be humbled into the dust...When England does declare war, all nations will have an interest of their own to serve, and there will be general war." (p. 259.) For awhile this is what seemed probable, and what was feared; but it never came.

Here, again, her prophecy was a complete failure. Our nation was not humbled into the dust. England did not declare war. All along it is clear that Mrs. White simply saw things just as circumstances at the time seemed to indicate, and wrote as those around her talked. If it had been true, as she claimed, that she was not writing any of this out of her own mind, but was simply recording what God told her, would he have told her that way?

Did not the Lord know that England would not declare war? Surely. If her predictions were not reliable then, they are not now. If she was not God's prophet then, she never was at any time.

Here is another blunder: "Had our nation remained united, it would have had strength; but divided, it must fall." (p. 260.) No such thing happened. It was not divided, nor did it fall. Did not the Lord know better than that? Yes. But she did not.

Mrs. White interpreted the Civil War as a sign of the end of the world, just as Adventists have been interpreting the European war. She says: "The scenes of earth's history are fast closing." (p. 260.)

Under the heading, "The Rebellion," she says: "The one all-important inquiry which should now engross the mind of every one is, *Am I prepared for the day of God?* Time will last a little longer." (p. 363.) Since then a generation has gone. Mrs. White, Elder White, and nearly all who then preached and heard that warning, are laid away. They needed no such warning, for they did not live to see that day, as she then predicted.

Failure, failure, failure is marked by ineradicable letters against all her predictions.

Notice now how she forbade her followers taking any part in sustaining the Government in the struggle to save the Union and free the slaves. "I was shown [that is, the Lord showed her] that God's people, who are his peculiar treasure, can not engage in this perplexing war, for it is opposed to every principle of their faith." (p. 361.) Hence not a single Seventh-day Adventist took any part in the effort to save the Union and free the slaves - not so much as to go as nurses. Had all the people done that way, the nation would have been divided, and slavery would be with us now.

During those dark days of the Civil War, Mrs. White privately warned our married people not to have any more children. Time was so short, and the seven last plagues were so soon to fall, that children born then would be liable to perish. But children born since then are now grandparents!

The horrors of the great Civil War, she, in her vivid imagination, interpreted as proof that the end of the world was right at hand, as already stated. In the same manner she interpreted the great war and revolution in Europe in 1848. It will be remembered that in that year there was quite a general war in Europe, in which several nations were engaged.

In January, 1849, Elder Bates published a pamphlet entitled "Seal of the Living God." He interpreted that it was as the beginning of Daniel's time of trouble (Dan. 12:1), and as fulfilling Rev. 11:18: "The nations were angry, and they wrath is come."

Her Prophecies Fail

On page 48 of his pamphlet he says: "The time of trouble, such as never was (Dan. 12:1), has begun." In proof of this he names several of the powers at war, thus: "Prussia, Hanover, Sardinia, Sicily, Naples, Venice, Lombardy, Tuscany, Rome, Austria," etc.

On page 15 he says: "And now the trouble has begun, what is our duty?"

On pages 24 and 26 he relates how, while he and others were discussing this question, Mrs. White had a vision in which she saw the same thing! She said: "The time of trouble has commenced, it is begun. The trouble will never end until the earth is rid of the wicked."

Elder Bates then says: "The above was copied word for word as she spoke in vision, therefore it is unadulterated."

Notice here, again, how she is influenced by Bates to see in vision just what he was arguing in her presence. Both were wrong.

Aug. 3, 1861, Mrs. White had a vision in which she was shown the Civil War, then just fairly begun. She says: "I was shown the inhabitants of earth in the utmost confusion. War, bloodshed, privation, want, famine and pestilence were abroad in the land." (*Testimonies*, Vol. I., p. 268)

This was exactly what all faultfinders at that date predicted–famine and pestilence. But nothing of this kind happened. There was no famine, no pestilence. Her predictions utterly failed. Where, then, did she get that "vision"? not from God, surely, but from the ideas of those around her, the same as she got all her "visions." The event proved this.

Claimed to Reveal Secret Sins

As usual with characters of this kind, extravagant and even superstitious views concerning Mrs. White have quite generally been held by the denomination recognizing her as its prophet and spiritual head. This was encouraged both by her own claims and by the teachings of her devout followers.

She claimed to be God's special messenger; to have been given the work of revealing and reproving "secret sins"; and to have been taken in vision from house to house and heard conversations which she was bade not to relate. Many of her followers looked upon her as endowed with supernatural powers, and went to her for counsel and advice as one would go to God himself.

Elder A.G. Daniells, president of their General Conference since 1901, in a statement made Feb. 12, 1914, said: "In my earlier ministry, when I was a young man, I thought Mrs. White knew everything about me; that she could read my thoughts." He had since learned better, and characterized his former views as "superstitious."

About the same time, Elder F.M. Wilcox, editor of the *Review and Herald*, their leading denominational paper, told how he felt when, while yet a boy, he first saw Mrs. White and heard her speak. He said: "I thought she could look right through me; that she knew everything I had ever done." He likewise characterized this as "superstitious."

Mr. Charles T. Shaffer, for a number of years elder of the first Seventh-day Adventists Church at Washington, D.C., in a statement dated Nov. 10, 1915, said: "I always considered Mrs.

White as the prophet of the Lord, and that all things were as open before her eyes and that she saw them as clearly as I can see a house through a glass window." He later learned that this was not so. She got her information from others.

One of Mrs. White's claims was that God had empowered her to know the thoughts and secrets of people without their knowledge, and then to reprove or expose them to save the church from hidden corruption. Hear her: "God has been pleased to open to me the secrets of the inner life and the hidden sins of his people. The unpleasant duty has been laid upon me to reprove wrongs and reveal hidden sins." (*Testimonies*, Vol. III., p. 314.)

Then she tells how she saw them in their homes, listened to their conversations, was in their councils, and heard all they privately discussed, just the same as God himself sees and hears and knows all this. Nothing could be hidden from her (*Testimonies*, Vol. V., p. 68.) Thus Elder Uriah Smith, in *Objections to the Visions Answered*, edition 1868, page 6, says: "They have exposed hidden iniquity, brought to light concealed wrongs, and laid bare the evil motives of the false-hearted."

URIAH SMITH

There is an abundance of evidence to disprove this claim. Numerous plain facts in her life refute it. Later, Elder Smith himself doubted this claim of Mrs. White's. Under date of March 22, 1883, he wrote me about his unbelief in her testimonies. I quote a few lines: "The cases of C------ and S----- are stunners to me." No wonder these cases were stunners to Smith, as they were to all of us. I knew both of these ministers well. But their sins were not revealed to Mrs. White, although she was closely associated with both of them.

Look at another case–that of Elder Nathan Fuller. Elder Fuller was a man of commanding appearance, large abilities, and was highly esteemed by the Advent people. There was a large church at Niles Hills, Pa. He lived near there, and for years had the oversight of this church.

About 1869 or 1870 Elder White and his wife visited this church and stayed at the home of Mr. Fuller. Elder White publicly praised Fuller as a godly man of much ability. Only a few days later, by the confession of a conscience-stricken sister in that church, it came out that for years Fuller had been practicing adultery with five or six of the women in the church. All of them confessed, and Fuller had to own it himself.

The community came near mobbing him. The whole denomination felt the shock and shame of it. But it hit Mrs. White the worst of all. She had been right there for days in Fuller's home, in meetings with him, had met all these women, yet knew nothing of all this rottenness. A little later I went there and held meetings for two weeks, met all these people, and learned the whole shameful story.

This case exposed the falsity of Mrs. White's claim that God revealed to her the "hidden sins" of his people. What could she say? As usual, after it was all common knowledge, she had a testimony telling all about it. It is printed in *Testimonies for the Church*, Vol. II., pp. 449-454.

She says: "The case of N. Fuller has caused me much grief and anguish of spirit." Yes, well it might, as it so forcibly exposed her own failure. To excuse herself, she says: "I believe that God designed that this case of hypocrisy and villainy should be brought to light in the manner it has been." That is,

God hid it from her and let the women expose it! If ever there was a case where her alleged "gift" of revealing "hidden sins" was needed, it was here—a widespread, awful, hidden iniquity, extending over years, and involving a whole church.

She had often met Fuller in general meetings, had been in his home, and had also met all these women. Yet she knew nothing about it at all. No wonder Smith was stunned.

The second case Smith mentioned was that of a minister far more prominent than Fuller. I was holding meetings in a church where this minister had shortly before also held meetings. The elder of the church and his wife told me how he had tried to seduce her, the wife, and had tried the same with a young sister, their adopted daughter. Inquiry revealed the fact that for a long time he had been at the same thing right along in other places.

I submitted these facts to the Conference, and he was deposed from the ministry. Mrs. White had been with him in meetings for weeks, and had been in the same church; yet she knew nothing about any of this. She was in total ignorance of it until after it all came out.

Later another case, a very bad one, came to light. A minister who had been one of their most trusted and valuable men came to Battle Creek one week before the General Conference was to meet there. He was to preach in the Tabernacle on Sabbath afternoon. His wife had long suspected his infidelity. So, searching through his trunk one day, she found hidden a bunch of letters from a woman which revealed their illicit intercourse. She informed the officials, and he was not allowed in the pulpit. At the conference I heard him confess his shame before several hundred in the Tabernacle.

Then, as usual, after it was out, Mrs. White had a testimony about it, entitled "The Sin of Licentiousness." I have that testimony now.

These cases show that her claim that God had commissioned her to reveal the "hidden sins" in the church are groundless. In all, I believe she wrote me fine personal testimonies during my ministry. I carefully scanned each one to see if there was any reference to anything in my life which none but God knew. There was never a word of such a thing in one of them. Any one well acquainted with me, as she was, could have told all she told.

Besides, she made several mistakes, supposing things to have happened which had not. Things like the foregoing narrated events, covering many cases, finally destroyed my confidence in her claims to divine revelations.

Several years before Mrs. White's death so many cases of immorality were discovered in one of their leading publishing houses that the institution was coming into disrepute in the community where it was located. Upon investigation, nearly a score of employees, among them some of the most faithful church-goers and tithe-payers, had to be dismissed for misconduct. Yet Mrs. White, their prophet, knew nothing about all this deplorable condition of things.

These cases, and many more which might be cited, are sufficient to show that her claim that God had commissioned her to reveal the "hidden sins" in the church was groundless. She had no such gift. As a revealer of secret sins she was a complete failure.

In this, as in many other things, she mistook her calling, and assumed responsibility which did not belong to her. Like the prophets of the Delphic Oracle in ancient Greece, she quietly and industriously gathered information from many sources about many things concerning which she was supposed to know little or nothing. Upon this she based many of her testimonies, which were represented as direct revelations from God. But, as with the Delphic prophets, in proportion as the true source of her information came to light, her "gift" fell into disrepute.

Influenced to Write Testimonies

That Mrs. White was influenced to write her testimonies to individuals by what others told her is easily proved. She denied this, and sought to make her followers believe that she received her information direct from heaven–that "the angel of God" had spoken to her and revealed their cases to her. (See *Testimonies*, Vol. III., pp. 314, 315; Vol. V., pp. 65, 683.)

But the facts to the contrary are too plain. Note the following illustrative examples:

REBUKED THE WRONG MAN

About the year 1882, two Adventists ministers, E.P. Daniels and E.R. Jones, were laboring together in Michigan. In giving a health talk one of them had made some remarks quite offensive to esthetic tastes. Not long afterward Elder Daniels received a testimony from Mrs. White, rebuking him for the offense, which she said took place at Parma, Mich. But, as the event turned out, she rebuked the wrong man, and the incident did not occur at Parma, but at another place.

Instead of Mrs. White acknowledging her mistake, Elder Daniels, the man wrongly accused, was induced to make the following statement: "Through a misunderstanding, I happened to be the person rebuked, in the place of the one for whom the rebuke was intended, and who justly merited it. Were all the facts known, it would leave no room for even the slightest disrespect for the motives that influenced her, as she has, as she supposed, the best of reasons for believing that her informant had told her the truth. And, indeed, he had, but he made a mistake in the name of the person. All that he had said was true of another, though the incident did not occur at Parma." (*Review and Herald Supplement*, Aug. 14, 1883, p. 10.)

At best this is "a lame apology for an inspired blunder." It demonstrates beyond question that in this instance at least Mrs. White was influenced to write the testimony in question by some one reporting to her; that her "informant" was not "an angel from heaven" speaking to her, as she had claimed, but an erring mortal; and that, between them, this "informant" and Mrs. White got things badly mixed up, both as to person and place.

When God rebukes a man he does not rebuke the wrong man. When he sent the prophet Nathan to David with the message, "Thou are the man," he hit the right man.

Continuing his explanation, Elder Daniels said: "Mrs. White told me plainly that this report came from a gentleman whose acquaintance they had formed when traveling in the West."

This again proves the falsity of her claim that she was not influenced to write testimonies by reports carried to her by various individuals. This testimony was written by Mrs. White while she was in Colorado. Had Elder Daniels, the one to whom it was addressed, been the guilty party, he probably would never have questioned its origin; and the church elders would have reasoned as they so often had reasoned in regard to other of her testimonies: "How could Sister White know so far away what Elder Daniels was doing at Parma, Mich., if the Lord had not shown it to her in vision?"

But the mistake revealed its origin. The best that could be done from Mrs. White then was to shift all the blame unto the man who gave her the report. In basing her communication as she did on the testimony of one man, she disregarded a plain principle laid down in the Bible: "Against an elder receive not an accusation, but before two or three witnesses." (1 Tim. 5:19.)

But this she did almost constantly in her testimony work. Her ear was ever open to hear reports. The writer was well acquainted with Elder Daniels. The mistake Mrs. White made in this case shook his faith in her testimonies, so much so that he came nearly leaving the work then. The writer had a long conference with him, trying to relieve his doubts; but they always stuck to him, and opened his eyes to other mistakes of Mrs. White. Finally, after years of struggle, he withdrew from the denomination, and opposes it now, the same as hundreds of other Adventist ministers, officials and honest laymen have done; and their numbers are bring added to constantly.

WHAT CALLED IT OUT

Take another case. For a number of years certain irresponsible and independent workers in the South made a practice of going among church members in some of the Northern states and collecting tithes and donations for their work. Elder George F. Watson, president of the Colorado Conference, objected to this being done in his conference. Before long he received a testimony from Mrs. White, dated Jan. 22, 1906, defending this irregularity, and admonishing him to silence.

In it she said: "It has been presented to me for years that my tithe was to be appropriated by myself...I have myself appropriated my tithe to the needy cases brought to my notice...It is a matter that should not be commented upon; for it will necessitate my making known these matters, which I do not desire to do...And if any person shall say to me, 'Sister White, will you appropriate my tithe where you know it is most needed?' I shall say, 'Yes,' and I will and have done so. I commend those sisters who have placed their tithe where it is most needed...For years there have been now and then persons who have lost confidence in the appropriation of the tithe who have placed their tithe in my hands...I have taken the money, given a receipt for it, and told them where it was to be appropriated. I write this to you so that you shall keep cool and not become stirred up and give publicity to this matter, lest more shall follow their example."

This communication from Mrs. White flatly contradicted what she had written ten years before. In the *Review and Herald* of Nov. 10, 1896, she had said: "Let none feel at liberty to retain their tithe to use according to their own judgment. They are not...to apply it as they see fit, even in what they may regard as the Lord's work...The minister...should not feel that he can retain and apply it according to his own judgment because he is a minister. It is not his...Let him not give his influence to any plans for the diverting from their legitimate use the tithes and offerings dedicated to God. Let them be placed in his treasury."

In 1909 this and other matters of similar import were gathered together and published in Volume IX of the *Testimonies.* At a General Conference committee council meeting held behind closed doors in Washington, D.C., Oct. 27, 1913, after reading these two contradictory statements, Elder Watson, holding up one in each hand, said he could not believe that both were written by the same person. He said he had charged J.E. White, Mrs. White's oldest son, with being the author of the 1906 communication; had told him he believed it was "a product of his own evil brain." For nearly eight long years he said he had been left in the dark as to whether it was a genuine testimony or not, and asserted that hundreds of thousands of dollars had been diverted from the regular channels by the use that had been made of it.

Finally, in that same meeting, Elder W.C. White, in response to what Elder Watson had said, made the following statement regarding it: "The letter was written by my mother, and was duplicated, and a copy was sent Brother Watson, and another copy, very unwisely I believe, and I am sorry to say, to my brother. What called it out was a letter from my brother to my mother. I am very sorry that the letter was written."

Notice some important facts:

1. Here we have two "inspired" testimonies from Mrs. White squarely contradicting each other.

2. She was influenced by one of her sons to write one of these, as the other son confesses. This disproves her claim that she was not thus influenced to write testimonies.

3. Notice also her duplicity. In her printed testimonies for the church she forbids others to use their tithes as they thought best. All must be strictly paid into the treasury. But she herself

INFLUENCED TO WRITE TESTIMONIES

used not only her own tithes, but those entrusted to her by others, just as she pleased, placing none in the treasury as she required others to do. Privately she encouraged confiding ones to send their tithes to her, contrary to her published testimonies.

When this was found out she admonished Watson to keep the fact concealed, lest she should be compelled to make an explanation, and others should be influenced to follow her example and the example of those whose course she commended! What shall we say of such manifest duplicity in a professed prophet of God?

4. If it was proper for one of her sons to be "sorry" for a testimony which she had been inspired to write by a letter she had received from the other son, why would it not be perfectly proper for the whole church to be sorry for many other things she was influenced to write in the same way?

All along Mrs. White was influenced in this way by her sons and by leading men in the denomination to write testimonies to individuals and churches. Both she and they tried to conceal the fact that her testimonies originated in this way.

In later years, some, like Elder A.G. Daniells, president of their General Conference since 1901, when desiring a testimony from her against some one, would write to her son, W.C. White, and he would read their communications to his mother. Then, when asked if they had written to Mrs. White about the individuals concerned, they would deny it, which was technically true, but false altogether in fact and effect, for they had written to her through her son. To such unworthy subterfuges both she and they resorted to shield her in her work and defend her testimonies. No gift, profession or observance prevented either her or them from practicing deception.

As early as 1867 Mrs. White herself admitted that she was influenced to write a testimony by letters received from the brethren. See latter part of the chapter, "Brief Sketch of Her Life," pages 77, 78. Of what use, then, was it for her to deny the fact in later years?

LED BY DR. KELLOGG TO DENY THE RESURRECTION OF THE BODY

All Adventists hold strongly to the material resurrection of the body which goes into the grave. In 1878, Dr. Kellogg advocated the theory that the dead body would never be raised, but that all that was left of a person at death was a record of his life kept in heaven. At the resurrection an entirely new body of new matter would be formed like the old one, and made to think that he was the same person as the old one! Dr. Kellogg influenced Elder James White to advocate this new view.

Kellogg presented his new theory before the General Conference, Oct. 8, 1878, and later published it in a book called *Soul Resurrection*. It met with strong opposition, but Elder White used all his influence for it. He invited Elder J.N. Andrews and myself to a private conference with himself and wife, hoping to win us to his side. But he failed to answer our objections.

Then he asked his wife is she had any "light" on the subject. She promptly declared that the Lord had showed her that not a particle of the old body would ever be raised, but that a new body of new material would be formed. I asked her how about Christ's body which was raised. She said he dropped it all when he ascended.

As the Lord had settled it, we dared say no more, though not convinced. Then she went before the conference and made the same positive statements as to what the Lord had "shown" her.

A young minister asked her how she reconciled her present statement with what she had written previously about angels "watching the precious dust of Wm. Miller." Of course she could not answer. Instead, she denounced the minister as a little upstart, and set him down summarily. The rest of us kept still.

Here we see how she was influenced by Dr. Kellogg and her husband to confirm what they wished. It illustrates how easily she was influenced, how readily she adopted any new or wild theory advocated by her associates, and how prompt she was to put upon it the stamp and sanction of divine inspiration and approval.

But this speculative theory about the resurrection did not take with the body of her people, so it was soon dropped. Notwithstanding Mrs. White's strong statements to the contrary, her church still believes and teaches the old doctrine of the resurrection of the material body which goes into the grave. This is only one of the many things which Mrs. White once taught as of divine revelation from God which her church no longer believes.

For many years in her published testimonies criticizing, reproving and accusing individuals, the names of the individuals were published; but this finally became so objectionable that in 1883, when her testimonies were revised, these names were omitted, and the persons referred to were indicated by letters of the alphabet. One of her testimonies incriminating a certain individual provoked a $50,000 suit for damages. The suit was settled out of court. But if it was proper for her to publish these names thus at first, why did she not continue to do so?

The omission of these names in this way is an open confession on the face of it that she was not inspired by God to put them in in the first place. Her "inspiration" to write these numerous and voluminous epistles came from another source, as has already been shown.

While she lived, every one in the denomination was liable to an attack, a cutting reprimand, or to dismissal from office from her if he chanced to be reported or complained of by someone to her. No one was safe from her ever ready and caustic pen. One denunciation from her meant a stigma on one's character and standing in the denomination for life.

She was at the same time both the dread and the idolized oracle of the denomination.

Broke the Sabbath Nine Years

Jews and Seventh-day Baptists keep the Sabbath as the Bible teaches, from sunset to sunset (Lev. 23:32; Mark 1:32.)

Elder Bates led Mrs. White and her husband to accept the Sabbath in 1846. He had been a sea captain, and by nautical time, began the day at 6 P.M. So he began the Sabbath that way. By him Mrs. White was led to keep it the same way until 1855–nine years.

In a pamphlet published at New Bedford, Mass., 1850, entitled *The Sabbath Controversy*, pages 80-82, Elder Bates wrote an article headed "The Beginning of the Sabbath." He says: "Here, also, we can not be too particular; God claims every moment of his day." Then he argues for the 6 P.M. time, and says: "Therefore by the same rule (and no other) we regulate the weeks, and must of necessity begin the Scripture day at 6 P.M."

In another pamphlet, entitled *The Sealing Message*, published in 1849, at the same place, he says: "Friday evening, 6 P.M., the Sabbath commences; all other figuring is lost time." (p. 38.) So Mrs. White blindly followed Bates in this unscriptural practice for nine years. This was not satisfactory to all, and a discussion arose over it. Some argued for sunrise time and some for sunset time. A division was feared. But Bates' influence was in the lead, and held them to 6 P.M.

In 1868, Elder U. Smith published a pamphlet entitled *The Visions–Objections Answered*, 144 pages. On page 90 he quotes Elder White thus: "Mrs. White has in two visions been shown something in reference to the time of the commencement of the Sabbath. The first was as early as 1847, at Topsham, Maine. In

BROKE THE SABBATH NINE YEARS

that vision she was shown that to commence the Sabbath at sunrise was wrong."

If the Lord gave her this vision, how natural and easy it would have been for him to tell her that sunset was the right time. Why simply tell her sunrise was wrong, and leave the whole church in error eight years more as to what time was right? The answer is easy. Bates was still in the lead, and opposed sunrise time, and she "saw" through his glasses; that was all.

In *Early Writings*, by Mrs. White, edition 1882, pages 25-28, is an account of this same vision at Topsham, Maine, 1847. She says: "I saw an angel flying swiftly to me. He quickly carried me from earth to the holy city." There she was taken by Jesus into the Holy of Holies and shown the ark. Jesus opened the ark and showed her the Ten Commandments. She says: "The fourth, the Sabbath Commandment, shone above them all...I saw that the holy Sabbath is, and will be, the separating wall between the true Israel of God and unbelievers." Then right along, page after page, she has vision after vision very frequently. She goes to heaven often, talks familiarly with Jesus and angels. She is told over and over about the Sabbath, how holy it is, and that it is the seal of God, and that people "are being tested on the Sabbath question" (p. 35.)

Why was she not told in some of these visits that she was beginning the Sabbath wrong, keeping part of two days? But not a hint of it was given her. How did she finally find out? This way:

A division among them was arising over this question. So Elder J. N. Andrews, the best scholar they then had, was requested to study the subject and present his conclusion to the conference held at Battle Creek, Mich., Nov. 16, 1855. This he did, and decided that sunset was the Scriptural time to begin the Sabbath. The conference voted to accept his view, and then the whole denomination changed from 6 P.M. to sunset, after nine years of error on this vital question. This is all told fully by Smith in The Visions–Objections Answered, pages 88-93.

Then, four days after Andrews and the conference had settled it, Mrs. White had a vision in which an angel told her that sunset was the right time! Smith says: "After the conference,

November 20, the vision was given, establishing those undecided on the sunset time." (p. 93.)

This put Mrs. White in a bad fix. So in that vision she complained to the angel and asked for an explanation. She says: "I inquired why it had been thus, that at this late day we must change the time of commencing the Sabbath. Said the angel, 'Ye shall understand, but not yet, not yet.'" (*Testamonies*, Vol. I., p. 116.)

That was over sixty years ago; Mrs. White is dead; but the promised explanation has never been given. So I will give it now: In her visions she saw just what Bates taught her. When Andrews had the lead, then she changed her views and saw just what he and the conference taught. That is the whole of it, and the like of that is the source of all her revelations.

Notice the importance of this blunder. For nine years they all began the Sabbath at 6 P.M. Friday. In June the sun at 6 P.M. would be two hours high when they began the Sabbath. They kept two hours of Friday, two hours on which they now work. At 6 P.M., with the sun two hours high on Saturday, they all went to work - plowing, washing, etc. They worked on two hours of the Sabbath, holy time as they now believe. In December it went the other way; they worked two hours on Friday after the Sabbath began, and kept two hours Saturday evening after the Sabbath ended!

So they actually broke the Sabbath every week for nine years. All this with Jesus and angels frequently talking with Mrs. White about the sacredness of the holy Sabbath! Did she not mistake Bates and Andrews for angels?

The Reform Dress

A Short Dress With Pants

One of the most manifest mistakes Mrs. White made was about what she called the "Reform Dress." Shortly before the Civil War of 1861-65 a few women wore and advocated a reform dress cut short–about half-way to the knees. With this they wore a sort of loose pants on the limbs below the dress.

Some Advent sisters favored it as convenient and healthful; but Mrs. White condemned it, with good reason, as follows: "God would not have his people adopt the so-called reform dress. It is immodest apparel, wholly unfitted for the modest, humble followers of Christ...Those who feel called out to join the movement in favor of woman's rights and the so-called dress reform, might as well sever all connection with the third angel's message...Let them adopt this costume, and their influence is dead...They [the sisters] would destroy their influence and that of their husbands. They would become a byword and a derision...God would not have us take a course to lessen or destroy our influence with the world." (*Testimonies for the Church*, Vol. I., pp. 421, 422.)

Notice that she gives God as her authority here. "God would not have his people adopt the so-called reform dress." That was God's mind at that date. Again she says: "If women would wear their dresses so as to clear the filth of the streets an inch or two, their dresses would be modest and they could be kept clean much more easily, and would wear longer. Such a dress would be in accordance with our faith." (p. 424.)

Notice the length of the dress–"to clear the filth of the streets an inch or two." Remember this.

Once more she says: "Christians should not take pains to make themselves a gazing-stock by dressing differently from the world." (p. 458.) Remember this also.

This was in 1863, and was clear and emphatic. But one year later, September, 1864, Elder and Mrs. White spent three weeks at Dr. Jackson's Health Home at Dansville, N.Y. Both were captivated with the new "Health Reform" taught there. Elder White wrote a flattering account of the institution and this system of health care.

Miss Austin, one of the physicians there, wore a "Reform Dress" with pants below the dress made like men's pants. Slightly modified, it was the same dress Mrs. White had condemned only a year before. But both she and her husband were captivated with it. Immediately she adopted it herself, and began to write revelations and testimonies to the sisters, saying God now wanted them to wear it.

It will be seen that after her visit with Miss Austin "the Lord" changed his mind on the dress question, for she says: "God would now have his people adopt the Reform Dress, not only to distinguish them from the world as his peculiar people, but because a reform in dress is essential to physical and mental health." (p. 525.)

Here, again, she gives God as her authority for the new departure in dress. This dress was to be adopted by sisters, not only for health, but to distinguish them from the world as God's peculiar people. She quotes Num. 15:38-41, where God directed the Israelites to wear a "ribbon of blue" on their garments to distinguish them from the other nations.

So now the Adventists women were to put on the reform dress so as to be peculiar from the world. This was the very thing she had condemned previously. She gave the exact length of the dress. She says: "I would say that *nine inches* as nearly accords with my view of the matter as I am able to express in inches." (p. 521.) In her testimony before visiting Miss Austin she expressly said *"an inch or two"* above the streets; but now it is *"nine"* inches. Measure nine inches from the floor and it will be about half-way up to the knee on a woman of ordinary

The Reform Dress

height. That was the way Miss Austin wore hers.

Mrs. White had patterns of the dress, coat, and pants cut out of paper. These she advertised in the *Review*, took with her wherever she went, and sold for one dollar each! She thus pocketed quite a nice sum of easy money. She strongly urged that these paper patterns of hers be obtained by all. She says: "I shall have patterns prepared to take with me as we travel, ready to hand out to our sisters whom we shall meet, or to send by mail to all who may order them. Our address will be given in the *Review*...Old garments may be cut over after a correct pattern...I beg of you, sisters, not to form your patterns after your own particular ideas." (p. 522.)

The only correct pattern was hers, the one she advertised in the church paper, carried with her everywhere she went, made out of cheap paper, and handed out to the sisters at only one dollar each! I was there, and that one dollar was the price. Many a poor sister who could ill afford it paid the dollar, and put on the pants.

I was married at Battle Creek in 1867, to a young sister of nineteen. It was at the height of this short-dress craze. Of course, as a minister's wife, she reluctantly put on the dress and wore it for eight years. So I know all about it.

It was a shameful thing, and brought ridicule everywhere. On the street, people would stop and gaze at her and mock. I have seen troops of boys follow her, making fun, till she would step into a store to hide from them. We were both ashamed of it; but God's prophet said it was his will, and we must bear the cross! Here is the warning Mrs. White gave: "I have done my duty; I have borne my testimony, and those who have heard me and read that which I have written, must bear the responsibility of receiving or rejecting the light given. If they choose to venture to be forgetful hearers, and not doers of the work, they run their own risk, and will be accountable to God." (p. 523.)

The issue was clear. Buy a pattern, cut off your dress, put on your pants, become peculiar, or reject the light, and meet the frown of God! So, quite largely, the faithful ones put on the dress. But it was a failure. The pants were hot in summer, and in winter the ankles were wet with snow. Husbands were mad, brothers would not go out with their sisters, and outsiders sneered and called them freaks. Girls with this dress on in school were avoided and ridiculed. But for eight years Mrs. White wore it and urged it.

I have often sat in the desk with her when she wrote it and preached on it as a Christian duty. If God ever gave her a revelation about anything, he did about that, for so she said strongly over and over. But at length she saw it was a mistake and a failure. So she went away to California and quietly laid it off herself, and never wore it afterward. Of course she was plied with requests for explanations; but she simply refused to give any. She said she had given the light. They could obey it or reject it. That was all!

The fact was, she had been misled by Miss Austin, and dared not own it, for she had said it was light from heaven, and had made God responsible for it all. Instead of assuming the responsibility for misleading the entire denomination on the subject, as she should have done, she threw the responsibility all on God, and blamed the sisters for abandoning the disgraceful and obnoxious custom, and for making it necessary for her to introduce "another less objectionable style." Here is what she wrote in 1875: "As our sisters would not generally accept the reform dress as it should be worn, another less objectionable style is now presented." (*Testimonies*, Vol. IV., p. 640.)

This is the course she took in shirking and shifting responsibility for an objectionable custom which she herself introduced and sought to impose upon her own people as a Christian duty. But if others disobeyed God in putting off this reform dress, so did she. When my wife discarded it she gave a great sigh of relief, and told me how she had always disliked it. Not one in the denomination wears it now, though there it stands in the "inspired testimonies" as the word and will of God.

This is only another illustration of the fact that Mrs. White in her revelations simply followed the lead of some one else, and was naturally inclined and easily influenced to take up with fanatical and extreme views, and advocate them as direct revelations from God.

Her False Vision About the Planets

As previously stated, Elder Joseph Bates first met Elder White and his wife in 1846. He was keeping the Sabbath, and urged it upon them. Neither saw any great importance in it at first, but nominally accepted it to please Bates, as it was important to gain his influence. Mrs. White was having visions which Bates did not believe were of God; but they were anxious to convince him that they were genuine.

Bates had been a sea captain, and had consequently studied the stars; had, in fact, become enthusiastic about astronomy. In the presence of Mrs. White and others he had often talked about the different planets, their positions, moons, and the "opening heavens."

In his book, *The Great Second Advent Movement,* page 260, Elder J.N. Loughborough, Mrs. White's great exponent and apologist, quotes a Mrs. Truesdale thus: "We all knew that Captain Bates was a great lover of astronomy, as he would often locate many of the heavenly bodies for our instruction."

Mrs. White seemed to pay no attention to the subject, or to have any interest in it. But soon she had a vision about the various planets, which is thus told by Loughborough on page 258 of his book just quoted: "One evening at the conference above mentioned [Topsham, Maine, 1846], in the house of Mr. Curtis, and in the presence of Elder (Captain) Bates, who was yet undecided in regard to these manifestations, Mrs. White, while in vision, began to talk about the stars, giving a glowing description of the rosy-tinted belts which she saw across the surface of some planet, and added, '*I see four moons.*' '*Oh,*' said Elder Bates, '*she is viewing Jupiter.*' Then, having made motions as though traveling through space, she began giving descriptions of belts and rings in their ever-varying beauty, and said, 'I see eight moons.' 'She is describing Saturn.' Next came a description of Uranus with his six moons, then a wonderful description of the 'opening heavens.'"

This was sufficient, and accomplished its purpose. Elder Bates was convinced, and became a firm believer in the visions.

But what are the facts? Mrs. White simply saw what her companions at the time generally believed and talked about. Had God given her that view about the planets and the number of moons to each he would have given her the correct number in each case, and thus she would have revealed what astronomers at the time did not know, but later discovered. This would have proved her vision to be of God. But, blundering as she did, proves that the Lord was not in it.

This vision was like all the rest of her revelations; she simply saw what others at the time had studied out and believed and talked about. Whether she pretended to see all this to win Elder Bates, or whether she really imagined she saw it, the fact remains that her statement of the number of moons to each planet was incorrect, and not in harmony with what we know to be the truth about them. Here, cold facts which cannot be denied prove her revelations to be wholly unreliable.

Here are the facts as compiled by E.E. Frank, of New York City: "Jupiter has nine moons instead of four; Saturn has ten moons instead of eight; and Uranus has only four moons instead of six."

These discoveries were made as follows:

JUPITER.

In 1892, Bernard, at Lick Observatory, discovered the fifth moon of Jupiter; in 1905, Perrine, at the same observatory, discovered the sixth and seventh; in 1908, Melotte discovered the eighth at Greenwich; and in 1914, Nickolson, at the Lick Observatory, discovered the ninth. Saturn. In 1899, Prof. W.H. Pickering discovered the ninth moon of Saturn, and in 1905, the tenth.

HER FALSE VISION ABOUT THE PLANETS

URANUS.

Sir Wm. Herschel discovered the two largest moons of Uranus, and supposed he had seen four others, which was believed up to 1851, five years after Mrs. White's vision. In 1851, Lassell positively proved that Uranus has only four moons. For these facts and the names of all these satellites see *Manual of Astronomy*, by Charles Young, Ph.D., LL.D., late professor of astronomy at Princeton University.

The conclusion is self-evident - Mrs. White's claim was false. She did not see Jupiter, for Jupiter has nine moons instead of four, as she said.

She did not see Saturn, for Saturn has ten moons instead of eight (seven), as she claimed to see.

She did not see Uranus, for Uranus has only four moons instead of six, as she claimed.

Any yet she represents that the Lord showed her all these things in vision. This vision of the moons, corresponding exactly with what Elder Bates believed, and convinced him the visions were of God. He asked her if she had ever studied astronomy, and she replied by saying that she did not remember ever having looked in a book on astronomy. That settled it with him. But she could easily have learned all this from his own previous conversations.

Later discoveries have now shown that both Jupiter and Saturn have more moons than she said. Elder Loughborough is obliged to confess this. In a foot note on page 258 of his book already quoted he says: "More moons to both Jupiter and Saturn have since been discovered." As a matter of fact, Mrs. White herself, relating this vision, described Saturn as having only *seven* moons, the number then assigned to that planet by astronomers.

Here are her own words in "Early Writings," page 32: "Then I was taken to a world which had *seven* moons." But by the time Elder Loughborough had written his book, *Rise and Progress of Seventh-day Adventists*, another moon had been discovered, and the publishers had the audacity to change her words to read, "I see *eight* moons." (See page 126 of that work.) This was in 1892.

When Elder Loughborough revised this book in 1905 and issued it under another title, still more moons had been discovered to this planet, hence his admission. The progressive discoveries of astronomy since Mrs. White had that vision have proved her revelation to be false. But it was a master stroke to win an influential convert to her cause. And it succeeded, fraudulent as it was.

Were Elder Bates alive today he would be compelled to reject her alleged vision of the planets as spurious, in view of her contradictions of known facts discovered since his death.

Revelations and visions which can be produced on demand or made to order to suit an occasion, may safely be questioned and distrusted, as well as may the peepings and mutterings of familiar spirits which come at a call.

J.N. LOUGHBOROUGH

"Give Sunday to the Lord"

From the first, Mrs. White taught that the Pope changed to Sabbath, that Sunday-keeping is "the mark of the beast," and that before the end, Seventh-day Adventists were to suffer great persecution because they would not cease working on Sunday. A decree was finally to go forth to slay them and rid the earth of them (*Early Writings*, pp. 29, 47, 55, 143, 145, ed. 1882.)

After a time, on account of their aggressive ways and their strong denunciations of those who observe Sunday, a few Seventh-day Adventists were imprisoned for short periods here and there for working on Sunday, and finally two of their publishing houses, one in London and one in Basil, Switzerland, were closed out for disregarding Sunday laws and laws regulating the hours of female labor. This set Mrs. White to thinking, and she finally had a revelation directing her people, the world over, to refrain from work on Sunday wherever the law requires it and prosecutions were threatened. They have all readily obeyed.

But, following this instruction, how, then, can they ever be persecuted for Sunday work?

In Australia there was a law requiring them to close their publishing house in Melbourne on Sunday. For three Sundays, after having had notice, they did not obey. Then they were threatened with arrest. What now? Did they brave the law and take the penalty as they had always said they would? Mrs. White, their divine oracle, fortunately was right there. Did she counsel martyrdom? Oh, no! She immediately produced a revelation directing them to obey the law, close the plant on Sunday,

AUSTRALIAN PUBLISHING HOUSE

and devote the day to the Lord in religious work just as Sunday-keepers do.

Here are her instructions in *Testimonies for the Church*, Vol. IX., No. 37, published in 1909. It is a square backdown from all she had published before. It avoids all possibility of persecution for Sunday work. She says: "The light given me by the Lord at a time when we were expecting just such a crisis as you seem to be approaching, was that when the people were moved by a power from beneath to enforce Sunday observance, Seventh-day Adventists were to show their wisdom by refraining from their ordinary work on that day, devoting it to missionary effort" (p. 232.) "Give them no occasion to call you lawbreakers." "It will be very easy to avoid that difficulty. Give Sunday to the Lord as the day for doing missionary work."

Further on she says: "At one time those in charge of our school at Avondale [Australia] inquired of me, saying, 'What shall we do? The officers of the law have been commissioned to arrest those working on Sunday.' I replied, 'It will be very easy to avoid that difficulty. Give Sunday to the Lord as a day for doing missionary work. Take students out to hold meetings in different places, and to do medical missionary work. They will find the people at home, and will have a splendid opportunity to present the truth. This way of spending Sunday is always acceptable to the Lord'" (p. 238.)

It will be readily seen that Mrs. White now directs her people to keep Sunday exactly as all conscientious Sunday observers do; that is, in holding religious meetings and doing religious work! They are to "refrain from their ordinary work on that day"; they are to "give Sunday to the Lord as a day for doing missionary work." And, to complete the somersault, they are told that "this way of spending Sunday is always acceptable to the Lord."

A prospect of arrest suddenly converted Mrs. White to a zealous religious observance of Sunday. "Give the day to the Lord."

And then especially notice: "This way of spending Sunday is always acceptable to the Lord." Good and true. Now, if it is acceptable to the Lord from Adventists, it must be acceptable to the Lord from Methodists, Baptists, Presbyterians, Congregationalists, and others. But the point is this: If Adventists follow this advice, how will they ever be persecuted for working on Sunday? What becomes of the prediction that an edict will be issued to kill them for violating a Sunday law? That is what Adventists have always taught before. But in 1909 they were directed to refrain from their ordinary work on Sunday, devote the day to religious exercises, and obey the law. If the prospect of simply a fine will cause Adventists to obey the law and refrain from work on Sunday, would not the prospect of a death penalty quickly induce them to obey? Surely.

It shows that their whole theory breaks down when put to a test.

Lastly, if Methodists, Baptists and other Christians have the mark of the beast because they "give Sunday to the Lord" in religious service, why will not Adventists also have it if they give the day to the Lord in the same way? Of course they will. If Sunday-keeping is the awful thing Adventists say it is, then what Mrs. White here tells her people to do is positively sinful - a compromise with sin. It is as if Daniel had said to his three Hebrew companions: "When the people are moved by a power from beneath to compel you to bow down and worship images, give them no occasion to call you lawbreakers. That difficulty can be easily avoided. You are to show your wisdom by devoting the time to prayer. Bow down, but while bowed pray to the God of heaven. That kind of worship is always acceptable to God."

In giving the instruction she did, Mrs. White herself removed the ground for the persecution under Sunday laws which she had previously predicted.

Conclusion

Mrs. White had much to say about the three messages of Rev. 14:6-10. These, she said, were the foundation of her message and movement.

The first, she held, was fulfilled in William Miller's time-setting movement of 1843-4.

For over sixty-five years she applied the second message, or fall of Babylon, to the Protestant churches, and said it could not apply to the "Romish Church." But, as we have seen, in 1911 she changed her teachings regarding this message, and applied it particularly to the Roman Church. If correct in her later exposition, she was in error, and taught error regarding the second message nearly all her life.

The third message warns against false worship and receiving the mark of the beast. Nearly all her life Mrs. White taught that the mark of the beast is Sunday-keeping; but, as we have seen from the preceding chapter, near the close of her life she changed her views regarding this, and said that to "give Sunday to the Lord" was always acceptable to him. In other words, she mistook and taught error regarding all three of the very messages which she and her followers have held to be the foundation of their movement. If wrong on the fundamentals, how can she safely be relied upon in other matters?

To summarize briefly some of her more prominent mistakes, the following may be noted:

She endorsed William Miller's time-setting of 1843-4.

She endorsed Captain Bates' time-setting for 1851.

She taught that there was no more salvation for sinners after

Oct. 22, 1844.

She suppressed some of her early visions and writings, and yet, in 1882, issued a book claiming to contain all of her early writings.

She predicted that the Civil War would be a failure, that the nation would be ruined, and that slavery would not be abolished.

She characterized Lincoln's proclamations for days of humiliation and prayer as "insults to Jehovah."

She taught a "reform dress" which made her followers a laughing-stock, and which she herself gave up after attempting to force it upon her church for eight years as a divine revelation and a religious duty.

She wrote against the eating of both butter and eggs.

She forbade the eating of meat, and said, "Can we possibly have confidence in ministers who, at tables where flesh is served, join with others in eating it?" (*Lake Union Herald*, Oct. 4, 1911), and yet secretly she herself ate meat more or less most of her life.

She taught her followers that they should not apply their tithes as they saw fit, but applied her own and those of others as she chose.

She denied having been influenced by letters or conversations in the writing of her testimonies, when the opposite was the fact.

She based many of her rebukes on mere hearsay reports, and, contrary to the Scriptures, upon the testimony of only one witness.

She claimed to have been divinely commissioned to reveal secret sins, but miserably failed in this. In numerous instances she rebuked the wrong man, and frequently accused individuals of doing things they had not done.

She seriously erred in her vision regarding the planets and the number of their satellites.

She plagiarized to such an extent that one of her books had to be suppressed altogether, and another had to be revised at an expense of $3,000.

In 1905 she promised to explain her mistakes and blunders,

Conclusion

and said that God would help her to do it; but in 1906 she said that God had told her not to attempt this.

One of the worst features of her life and writings is that she was always making God responsible for her mistakes and failures.

Her worst deception, as that of her followers, was to mistake her unfortunate affliction of epilepsy and epileptic fits as divine revelations and visions from God. Mrs. White not only claimed that her writings are the "testimony of Jesus" and the "spirit of prophecy" referred to in Rev. 12:17 and Rev. 19:10, but she firmly held that she and her followers are the 144,000 of Rev. 7:1-4 and Rev. 14:5, although their present adult membership is over 150,000.

The great characteristic of the 144,000 as described in the last named Scripture is that "in their mouth there was found no guile." Guile is deception. No guile, therefore, means no deception. But, as pointed out in so many instances in this book, Mrs. White's claims to being an inspired prophet of God have been maintained very largely by deception, both on her own part and on the part of her defenders and supporters. Both she and they, therefore, fail to meet the very description and characteristic which Inspiration has seen fit to give of the 144,000.

No genuine gift of God, no true gift of the Spirit, has ever required guile–deception, deceit, fraud, or double-dealing–to defend and sustain it.

That she meant to be a Christian, and that her works contain many things good in themselves, need not be denied. Her motives we may safely leave with God. But her high claims are not defensible. They are disproved by too many patent and incontrovertible facts.

www.ingramcontent.com/pod-product-compliance
Lightning Source LLC
LaVergne TN
LVHW020254180225
803988LV00007B/378